We love because he first loved us.

—1 John 4:19 (NIV)

MYSTERIES *of* BLACKBERRY VALLEY

Where There's Smoke
The Key Question
Seeds of Suspicion
A Likely Story
Out of the Depths
Run for the Roses
Crooks and Christmas Cookies
Smoke and Mirrors
No Love Lost
The Cookbook Clue
The Final Cut

MYSTERIES *of* BLACKBERRY VALLEY

The Final
Cut

ROSEANNA M. WHITE

Guideposts

A Gift from Guideposts

Thank you for your purchase! We want to express our gratitude for your support with a special gift just for you.

Dive into *Spirit Lifters*, a complimentary e-book that will fortify your faith, offering solace during challenging moments. Its 31 carefully selected scripture verses will soothe and uplift your soul.

Please use the QR code or go to **guideposts.org/ spiritlifters** to download.

Mysteries of Blackberry Valley is a trademark of Guideposts.

Published by Guideposts
100 Reserve Road, Suite E200
Danbury, CT 06810
Guideposts.org

Cover and interior design by Müllerhaus
Cover illustration by Bob Kayganich at Illustration Online LLC.
Typeset by Aptara, Inc.

ISBN 978-1-965859-05-6 (hardcover)
ISBN 978-1-965859-06-3 (softcover)
ISBN 978-1-965859-07-0 (epub)

Printed and bound in the United States of America
10 9 8 7 6 5 4 3 2 1

The Final Cut

Chapter One

Hannah Prentiss picked up two plates of pie and trailed her best friend into the living room of the Minyard home, smiling to see her boyfriend, Liam, and Lacy's husband, Neil, laughing over something. She handed one of the pie plates to Liam and settled beside him on the couch.

Lacy sat too, rubbing a hand over the baby bump beginning to show in earnest. "Mm, pie," she said. "Baby approves."

Everyone laughed, and Hannah dug into the coconut cream confection she'd chosen from the variety they'd pooled together for their Easter Monday leftover extravaganza. "I agree with Baby."

A comfortable silence fell as they took their first bites, though Neil broke it a moment later, eyes going wide. "Oh, hey. Have you guys heard about the film crew coming to town? Ford Payne told me about it when I ran into him today. Apparently, they booked his old farmhouse to stay in."

Liam paused with a bite of key lime halfway to his mouth. "I haven't. What kind of film crew?"

"A television show called *Destination Discovery* is going to film an episode here. You guys ever watch it?"

Hannah choked on her pie.

Liam, his attention on Neil, said, "Sure, I've caught quite a few episodes. Ryan Hall's one of my favorite TV hosts. I like his sense of humor. And the show's always interesting, especially when he's doing archaeological stuff." As Hannah struggled to recover, he rubbed her back. "You okay?"

Hannah managed a laugh that turned into a cough. "I'm fine. Seriously, Neil? Ryan's coming to town?"

The other three went still, probably at how familiarly she'd said his name.

Lacy arched her brows. "Are you on a first-name basis with Ryan Hall?"

Hannah laughed again and wiped the cough-induced moisture from her eyes. "Yeah, actually. I met him in LA. I guess it was about seven years ago now. He hadn't pitched *Destination Discovery* yet. He was still hosting his first show, *Uncover the Unknown*."

Neil frowned. "I don't think I've ever seen that one. It was about weirder stuff, wasn't it? Cryptids and ghosts—that sort of thing?"

Hannah cleared her throat again. "Yeah, it was. I watched a few episodes because they went to some fascinating places all over the world to investigate the strange stories people sent them. But Ryan always approached it very logically, despite the premise. He told me that God is full of mysteries and who's to say what wonders He made that we haven't yet discovered or don't understand?" She shrugged. "Not that I think the chupacabra is really out there, but far be it from me to put God in a box."

Liam set his empty plate on an end table and turned to face her. "So how did you meet him? At the restaurant where you worked?"

"Yeah." She set her fork down on her plate. "He came in with some of his crew, which included a friend of mine from church, Kayla Dreher. I'd gone out to do my nightly walk-through of the restaurant to see how everyone was enjoying their meals, and stopped to say hello to Kayla. I honestly didn't even recognize Ryan. But they invited me to join them for ice cream after my shift was over, and I agreed." She shrugged. "We ended up doing quite a few things together when they were in the States, though the crew traveled almost constantly."

"Wait." Lacy leaned forward. "Do you mean 'we' as in you and the whole crew, or 'we' as in you and Ryan Hall?"

"Both, I guess. Mostly the group, but Ryan and I had dinner together once."

"You dated Ryan Hall?" Lacy squealed. "And you never told me?"

Hannah laughed. "There was nothing to tell. We weren't *dating*. One date, nothing ongoing. We got along well, but between my schedule and his traveling, we both knew it was far from the right time for anything like that. And then—well, you know how seasons of things go. I couldn't make one of the group meet-ups, then they relocated to New York for a year to be closer to one of the production companies or something." She shrugged. "Long story short, I haven't heard from him in six years, but I'd still call him a friend. Frankly, I don't think he's ever met anyone he *wouldn't* call a friend."

That was the kind of guy Ryan was—charming and funny and always growing his contact list.

Lacy pursed her lips, then said, "So you haven't kept in touch?"

Hannah shook her head. "Not really, no. The occasional comment on social media. I still keep in touch with Kayla though." She frowned. "I'm kind of surprised she didn't tell me they were coming here. She knows I moved home."

"Maybe she wanted to surprise you." Neil set his empty pie plate on the end table too.

Lacy gave an exaggerated sigh. "My best friend dated a television star. So cool."

Hannah laughed. "He wasn't a star at the time, and as I said, we weren't dating. One dinner."

"I'm totally counting that." Lacy's gaze shifted to Liam, and amusement sparkled in her eyes. "Liam does too. Right, Liam?"

Hannah turned her head to look at him better. He slid an arm around her, and warmth entered his gaze. "His loss. My gain."

She grinned back and forked up another bite of pie.

The conversation shifted to other things for the rest of the visit, but after they'd said their farewells to the Minyards and Liam walked Hannah to her car, she returned to the topic. "If the *Destination Discovery* crew is in town long enough, maybe I can get them to come to the restaurant sometime. I could introduce you. I bet you and Ryan would hit it off. And I'd love to see Kayla again."

In the light of the setting sun, Liam's smile was charmingly crooked. "You can't blame me if I'm a little jealous, right? I mean, it's *Ryan Hall.*"

Hannah chuckled and slid her arms around his waist, giving him a long hug. "Jealous I know him and you don't, you mean?"

He laughed and pressed a kiss to the top of her head. "Sure. That's it."

She tilted her face toward his. "He's every bit as funny and charming in real life as he is on screen. But I have to say, I prefer the hometown hero sort of guy. I'll take a fire chief over a travel show host any day of the week."

Eyes twinkling, Liam leaned down for a soft kiss. "Good to know. Because the fire chief has no intention of letting you go. And

I'd enjoy meeting your old friends, if you can arrange it. I hope you get the chance to reconnect with them."

Hannah gave him one more kiss. "I'll see what I can do. Talk to you tomorrow."

Liam opened her car door for her, then went to his Jeep. Soon they were each on their way down the driveway. Hannah soaked in the signs of spring that painted the landscape with fresh color as she drove, smiling anew at the gorgeous sunset that doused the clouds in pinks and oranges and purples as she reached town.

Once home and settled, she took out her phone and opened a social media app, intending to pull up Kayla's contact info and send her a message. When she saw one already waiting from her old friend, she grinned and opened it.

Hey, Han! You'll never guess what I did. I found a mystery for Ryan to investigate right in your hometown. How cool is that? I would have reached out sooner, but we just got it all finalized today and will be arriving tomorrow. The usual whirlwind. We carved out ten days to be there before we need to leave for Peru, and we'll have to do quite a bit of our research on location. Will you be in town? Please say yes, or I will have done all this work for nothing. Ryan and Oran and I would love to get together with you. Let me know how we can make that happen.

Hannah plopped down on her couch and reread the message, still smiling. If this show was anything like the one Kayla, Ryan, and Oran Murray—a camera operator who'd been on Ryan's first crew—had been working on seven years ago, there were always a lot of irons in the fire, and the choice of which they devoted time to was often a matter of what fit between other projects with an allotted budget. They were constantly flying off to who-knew-where with little notice when things suddenly lined up or other plans fell through.

No doubt an investigation in Barren County, Kentucky, would be a cheap and easy show, leaving more budget available for things like that trip to Peru. But she had a feeling Kayla had been looking for a mystery worth investigating in Blackberry Valley ever since Hannah told her she was moving home. Her friend had often joked that in order to travel wherever she wanted to go next, all she needed to do was find a compelling mystery for Ryan to film.

Hannah pulled up her schedule for the next two weeks. With Easter behind her, she didn't have much outside the normal weekly activities to intrude on her time. She typed her reply.

So good to hear from you, Kayla! I just heard that the show is coming to town and was hoping you'd be coming with them. What are you guys investigating? If I can be of any help, let me know. I could hook you up with locals who might have information you'll be looking for, at the very least.

And I would love to get together with you all. I can introduce you to Liam, my boyfriend. He's the fire chief and a big fan of the show. I know he and Ryan will get along great. Let me know when you get here, and we'll sort out the details. I hear you've rented a house on the outskirts of town for your stay. That should give you a good taste of the area. And speaking of taste, you guys have to come eat at the Hot Spot at least once.

She hit send, and within a minute, the dancing bubbles showed her that Kayla was online and typing her reply. It popped up soon after.

We'll be hunting for a stolen diamond that we suspect was stashed somewhere in your area in 1910. Franklin Sullivan, a Chicago anarchist, stole it from one of his compatriots in Arkansas. I found documentation of him being in Blackberry Valley to hide out at his sister's place, and get this—the vacation rental we booked used to be her house! We were able to get permission to film there, which is going to make this so much fun. Don't suppose you just happen to know the real history?

Hannah laughed and typed her reply.

If only. I've never even heard of it. But I can't wait to see what you all find.

Kayla promised to let her know when they got in the next day. After sending a thumbs-up emoji, Hannah set her phone down and reached for the TV remote. She hadn't watched any of *Destination Discovery* since she moved home, given that she was always at the restaurant when it was on. She had set it up to record but hadn't gotten around to watching the recordings yet.

She pulled up one of the episodes, in which the team traveled to Europe to hunt for treasure stolen by the Nazis. A lot of television shows like Ryan's never found answers to the mysteries they investigated, but Ryan actually did. That was what she'd really admired about his new show when she watched the first couple of seasons. He found quite a few things that had been lost to history, which had in turn gained him a reputation in the archaeology community.

Now people invited his crew to record when they unsealed tombs or got permission for an excavation or discovered a new lost city in the rainforest. She sometimes wondered, in fact, if some of the invitations came because Ryan brought gear and technology with him that they needed and didn't have access to, thanks to his having a major television network backing him and footing the bill.

She smiled when the Ryan on her screen brushed away some dirt and let out his catchphrase, "No *way*!" He said it enough in real life that it had worked its way into every episode of every show he'd been a part of, but it still made her laugh. When she commented on it once, he said that he was now contractually obligated to utter that phrase at least three times per episode. A joke? Maybe, maybe not. Contracts could be bizarre in Hollywood.

It was a little strange to think that part of her old life in LA would be appearing here, in a world so far removed from the hustle and bustle of the big city. But she couldn't wait to see Kayla again and to reconnect with Ryan and Oran.

A search for a long-missing diamond? She smiled once more at the thought. That sounded like fun. If she was lucky, they'd let her tag along. She wasn't about to be left out of solving this mystery on her own home turf.

Chapter Two

Hannah accepted a square of savory pastry from her chef, Jacob Forrest, then held it up to admire the flakiness and color of the crust and the contrast of the cheese sauce and the asparagus spears.

A long inhale came next, even though she'd been smelling his latest creation all morning as he experimented with a new menu featuring the bounty that was currently in season. It was lunchtime, but that wasn't the only reason her mouth watered. The aroma of puff pastry, cheese, shallot, and fresh asparagus was just that good.

Finally, she took a bite. She closed her eyes to better savor it, letting the flavors mix on her tongue. A happy groan escaped, and she couldn't regret it when she opened her eyes to see Jacob's grin. She finished chewing and swallowed before saying, "This is awesome. Seriously. Got a name for it?"

"I was thinking 'A Taste of Spring Tart.' What do you think?"

She took another bite. "What cheeses are in here? Is that gruyere?"

"And fontina."

"It's a great blend. And nutmeg?"

"Just a pinch, and some lemon zest." Jacob motioned to a cooling rack that held a rather strange-looking pie. "And while I was making puff pastry anyway, I gave that a go."

Hannah polished off the last bite of tart and moved in for a closer look at the pie. "Okay, I'm going to need some more information."

Jacob chuckled and reached for a knife, pie server, and two plates he had sitting nearby. "It's an Italian rice pie. Puff pastry shell, orange-ricotta filling, and short-grain rice. Sweet, not savory."

"Interesting." Hannah waited while he sliced into it and lifted two pieces onto the plates.

He handed one to her, along with a fork, and kept one for himself. "I've yet to try it either, though I tasted the filling, of course. Ready?"

She cut off a bite in answer, waited for him to do the same, and they both lifted their first tastes to their lips at the same time. The combination of creamy ricotta, aromatic orange and vanilla, and the delicate flake of the crust hit all the right notes. "Oh, yeah. This is going on the menu."

"What do you think of 'Orange Dreams Pie'?"

"Love it—both the name and pie. So good." As she chewed another bite, her phone buzzed with the arrival of a text. Seeing Kayla's name on the screen, she smiled. "Ah, they're here! I'm going to let them in." She'd already told Jacob that she was letting the crew of *Destination Discovery* come in before opening, to welcome them and say hello.

He turned back to the fryer. "I'll bring out some appetizers for them in a few."

"Thanks." She knew Kayla and Ryan wouldn't expect any food before opening, much less on the house, but she didn't want to welcome her friends to her restaurant and not feed them something. So she and Jacob had agreed to offer a sampling of their appetizers, along with Sparkling Spring Tea, the fizzy lemon-flavor black tea they'd just added to the menu.

As she strode out of the kitchen and toward the front doors, her own level of excitement surprised her a little. It had nothing to do with the cameras and sound gear she saw the crew unloading from the van parked outside the restaurant. She'd been around Ryan's first crew enough to know that they filmed everything, so they had some "local flavor" to add to the final edit. And in case Ryan said something amusing that just had to go into the show. No, Hannah's excitement was due to the brunette woman bouncing on her toes and waving wildly.

"Kayla!" She hadn't realized how much she'd missed her friend until they collided in a laughing embrace. They'd always had the kind of friendship that would let them go long stretches without any communication and then pick up where they'd left off—a requirement when one of them constantly jetted around the world.

Kayla gave her a hearty squeeze. "It's so good to see you, Hannah."

"Hey, there's our girl."

Hannah scarcely had time to glance over Kayla's shoulder before a bear of a man swooped in and wrapped his arms around them both.

She laughed again as he tried to squeeze the life out of them. "Hi, Ryan." She had forgotten how big he was, both in stature and in presence.

He stepped back, his trademark boyish grin in place. "I'd ask how you've been, but you look great. And what's more, something smells awesome." He turned to the door, where three others—one of them Oran, the camera operator, who grinned at her—jockeyed their gear inside. "I wish we had a way to transmit aromas to the viewer. Seriously, what is that? I can't decide if I'm smelling cheese or piecrust."

"Both, actually." Hannah tugged Kayla out of the way of the crew and motioned to a table in the empty restaurant. She glanced outside to see if that was all of them. A striking, vaguely familiar woman walked by. Hannah thought she might be with the film crew, but the woman went on, though she watched them curiously.

Well, curiosity was to be expected when a camera crew was around. Rather than try to figure out who the woman was—she *knew* she'd seen her before but couldn't place where—Hannah waved a hand toward the tables. "Come in, sit. My chef's getting some appetizers ready for everyone. And if you want some of his newly created Taste of Spring Tart that you're smelling, I'm sure that can be arranged too."

Still grinning, Ryan slung an arm around Hannah's shoulders. "Yeah, I've missed you."

Hannah snorted. "You mean you've missed my food."

"Same thing." He let his arm drop with a wink and then motioned to the crew. "We can film here, right? For our 'local flavor' bit? Kayla will get you a release to sign. But first, introductions. You remember Oran." He indicated the other member of his crew Hannah already knew.

Oran, a short, balding man who was peering into his view-finder, gave a wave. "Hi, Hannah."

Hannah smiled. "Still coming at the world lens-first, I see." She'd teased him endlessly about that, once upon a time. The group never went anywhere without a camera. At first she thought it was Ryan's hubris, but it hadn't taken long to realize that Oran simply saw things best with a camera in his hand. "Good to see you again, Oran."

Ryan motioned to a short woman with a dyed-white pixie cut who carried a shaggy microphone on a boom pole. "Lexi Stokley, our resident sound engineer extraordinaire."

Lexi gave a little salute and a crooked smile. "Hey."

"Good to meet you, Lexi," Hannah said.

"And Lexi's husband, Trevor Stokley, on camera two."

Trevor waved at Hannah around his camera. "Kayla's told us how awesome you are. And Ryan has talked endlessly about your cooking."

Laughing again, Hannah nodded a hello to Trevor and sent a playful scowl Ryan's way. "He knows his priorities. I'll give him that."

Ryan splayed his hand over his chest. "My praise was totally relevant. Kayla tried to lure us in with talk of obscenely large diamonds, but I know the *real* way to my crew's heart."

"It's true," Lexi said. "I keep telling him we're only in it for the food we get to sample everywhere we go."

"For real," Trevor agreed. "You haven't lived until you've had street food in Marrakesh."

The show did seem to include a marketplace scene in nearly every episode, with Ryan sampling whatever food the area was known for. And she'd always loved that they often broke the unwritten rule about the crew staying out of the shot, so that the viewer could see them enjoying it too. People who ranked food above industry standards were her kind of people.

"Well, I can't take full credit for what you're about to sample. I have a hand in it, but it's mostly the work of my amazing chef, Jacob." Why was Kayla grinning at her like that? "What?"

Kayla shook her head, sending her bob swaying. "It's just so good to see you again. I was beginning to think I'd have to take a trip here on my own dime, until I found that diamond story."

"Oh, her scheming has gone well beyond that." But Ryan's expression said he approved of whatever measures Kayla had taken.

Hannah lifted her brows. "Scheming?"

Kayla glanced at Ryan, then back to Hannah, still grinning. "Well—"

"Anyone hungry?" Jacob emerged from the kitchen, a large tray balanced on each hand.

Hannah rushed forward to take one from him. The crew responded enthusiastically, actually putting down their equipment in favor of sitting at the tables. Unsurprisingly, Jacob had added the new dishes they'd been testing to the appetizers they'd already decided to offer. Hannah should have known she wouldn't have to ask him.

"Figured we might as well get more opinions," he said to her. "Since we've been surprised by the reception of dishes before."

She didn't point out that these LA natives wouldn't exactly be representative of their small Kentucky town's inhabitants. Feedback was feedback. "They were eager to try what they smelled, so good call."

Ryan stood with his hands resting on the back of the chair beside Kayla, delivering a story into Oran's camera. About Hannah's cooking and his first experience with it back in LA, apparently. "...and then I tasted the mashed potatoes. They're just mashed potatoes, right? Standard fare, I thought. But that's when I found out that the mistake with that other reservation had been a gift from

God, and that Kayla was absolutely right about insisting we try out her friend's place."

Hannah slid the plates from tray to table. "It wasn't my place, just my kitchen." A distinction she knew Jacob would understand, but which she doubted the rest of them would. A head chef had a certain amount of investment in a restaurant, to be sure, but while they ran the kitchen, they didn't run the establishment. They didn't make final decisions or decide on themes or have the authority to make changes.

This was her place, and this kitchen was Jacob's.

Ryan pointed a finger at her. "They were your mashed potatoes."

She chuckled. "True." Her gaze moved to Kayla, who watched Ryan with a strange look in her eyes. Part amusement, part…something else, something more serious. But Kayla's expression shuttered before Hannah could name it. "I didn't realize you came that night knowing it was where I worked. I thought you just happened by."

"Are you kidding?" Kayla asked. "You'd mentioned a couple weeks earlier in Bible study that you were a chef, and I was dying to come by and get a taste. I was waiting for my chance." She slapped Ryan playfully on the arm. "This one used to always insist on making the reservations though, as the resident foodie. Didn't trust my taste."

"In my defense," Ryan said, finally pulling out the chair and sitting, "you have horrible taste four times out of five."

Kayla laughed brightly enough that it was clear she took no offense. "It's not my taste. I never like the places I pick either. I get sucked in by hype. But Hannah's restaurant was that one out of five."

"And her suggestions got a lot better after she started recommending places Hannah recommended to her," Oran chimed in, passing the stack of small plates to his colleagues without taking his eyes from the appetizers Jacob had set on the table. "This all looks awesome."

Ryan pulled out the remaining empty chair beside him. "You're joining us, right?" he asked Hannah.

"Absolutely."

"Let's say grace." Kayla put her hands on the table, palms up, reaching one toward Ryan and the other toward Oran.

It was good to see some things never changed. Kayla had always been the one to insist on saying grace, no matter which group she was with—and in LA, they were often in very mixed company. Clearly this crew was used to it. They joined hands without a protest, Hannah taking the hands of Ryan and Lexi, who sat on either side of her.

Jacob picked up the empty trays. "I'll be back out with the tea in a minute," he told her quietly.

"Thanks, Jacob."

Kayla blessed the food and thanked God for this opportunity, asking Him for a trip not only productive but full of fellowship with old friends and the chance to make some new ones.

Hannah found herself smiling as she chimed in on the amen, not only because of the heartfelt simplicity of the prayer, but because both Ryan and Lexi gave her hand a squeeze. Another habit Kayla had clearly passed along.

It had been too long since she'd seen her friend. It was too easy to forget the little things that made Kayla special when they'd been apart for so long.

Jacob returned with another tray. He passed out glasses of ice, then asked, "Who wants our sparkling lemon tea, and who wants water? Or if someone prefers soda, we can do that too."

Everyone but Oran, who couldn't have caffeine, opted for the tea, and Hannah grinned as they took their first sips and promptly exclaimed over it. The tea had been her creation rather than Jacob's, so it was nice to hear that it was well received.

Jacob hovered at the end of the table for a moment, smiling his professional chef's smile. "Can I get anyone anything else? Something more substantial than the apps, maybe?" He shot a glance Hannah's way.

She nodded her approval. They'd only discussed complimentary appetizers and drinks, but he knew her well. If her friends were hungry, she would feed them.

Kayla shook her head. "This is great," she said. "There's more than enough here to be lunch for us all."

"Okay," Jacob said. "But if anything changes, say the word, and I'll be happy to whip up anything you want. Otherwise, I'll be baking cookies."

"Cookies?" Lexi paused with her hand hovering over fried cheese curds. "You've found my weakness."

Her husband laughed, draped an arm along the back of her chair, and rubbed her shoulder. "Every dessert is her weakness."

"But especially cookies," Lexi said.

Jacob grinned. "I'll bring some as soon as they come out of the oven. You all enjoy."

Hannah shook her head when Ryan offered her a plate. The tart and pie had been enough for her, though she did pour herself a glass of tea and watched their reactions as everyone dug in.

Well, almost everyone. Ryan watched his crew too, rather than raising a bite to his own lips, which made her frown. He was usually the first to get the food from plate to mouth, often with Oran's camera pointing at him.

This must be something the crew had already discussed, though, because they each took their first bites and then looked at Ryan, nodding with enthusiasm.

"Awesome," Trevor declared.

"Amazing," Lexi added.

"As expected." Oran moved his smile from Ryan to Hannah.

"Told you so," Kayla said, leaning back in her chair to wink at Hannah.

Hannah lifted a brow. "Why do I get the feeling the Hot Spot just passed some sort of test?"

Ryan laughed. "Because you have. Kayla and I thought we'd ask you to do craft services for the show while we're here, but we agreed it would have to be a unanimous decision."

"We've had a few bad experiences," Lexi said, wincing. "No offense, of course. We figured Kayla and Ryan's chef friend would know her stuff, especially since they've had your food before, but it's never a guarantee. I'm sorry to say that when we hired my cousin, who has a catering company, it was a complete disaster."

Hannah's lips parted, but it was a long moment before she found words. "Craft services?" She looked from Lexi to Ryan and then beyond him to Kayla, who still grinned at her. "As in, all the food for you guys while you're in town?"

"You helped on a production or two in LA, didn't you?" Kayla asked.

"Yeah. And it was fun." Keeping a table stocked with quick and convenient snacks for people to grab as they needed them, plus providing meals, was a fun challenge. Most productions' craft services didn't provide full meals, but Ryan usually requested them for days they weren't going to film anything at a local eatery. Hannah had never been the head of craft services before, but she'd been on a team and had enjoyed the behind-the-scenes view of the filmmaking process it provided.

Still, she lifted her brow. "You *do* know this food is Jacob's creation, not mine, right? Is it me you want to hire, or my chef?"

Ryan laughed. "You, if you can get away. We thought it would be a good way to spend time with you while we're in town. Assuming Jacob and the rest of your staff can hold the fort here for ten days?"

Spotting movement at the entrance to the kitchen, Hannah looked up to see Jacob standing there, a smile on his face and giving her a thumbs-up. She smiled too. "They can, yes. I mean, I'll still have to take care of the ordering and stuff like that, but those are things I can do outside of production hours." It would mean a jam-packed ten days, having to be at their base of operations from before breakfast until after dinner, then coming back to the Hot Spot to take care of the things only she could handle. But it would be worth it for time with her friends. "I'm in."

"Yay!" Kayla clapped her hands around a crostini topped with brie, fig, and prosciutto. "And you should see if your friend can help you, since I missed out on meeting her when she visited you in LA. Tracy, is it?"

"Lacy." Hannah took her phone from her pocket. "I have a feeling she'll be eager to help out. She and her husband are big fans of the show." She wasn't about to share Lacy's reaction to the news that Hannah had "dated" Ryan, not with Ryan sitting right there.

Kayla nodded. "And I need to meet this fire chief boyfriend of yours too. From the stories you've posted online, he seems great. I mean, a handsome fire chief is a little cliché, but—"

Hannah laughed, knowing her cheeks probably looked as pink as they felt. "You'll like him, I'm sure. Liam's amazing."

Was it her imagination, or did Ryan go stiff beside her?

When she glanced at her phone, she saw a message from Marshall Fredericks, which was odd. Raquel's boyfriend didn't often text *her*. But she'd look at that later.

She scrolled to her message thread with Liam, smiling at the name he'd given himself two weeks before—Liam "My Love" Berthold. It only took her a moment to type a quick message to him. HEY, YOU'LL NEVER GUESS WHAT HAPPENED. KAYLA AND RYAN ASKED ME TO PROVIDE THE FOOD FOR THEIR CREW WHILE THEY'RE IN TOWN. THEY SAID THEY WANT TO MEET YOU. MAYBE YOU COULD LEND A HAND IN YOUR OFF-HOURS SO WE'LL HAVE TIME TOGETHER?

She pulled up her text thread with Lacy next and dashed off the invitation to join in on the fun.

She no sooner sent it than a reply came from Liam. NICE! I KNOW YOU'LL ENJOY THE TIME WITH YOUR FRIENDS, AND OF COURSE I'LL HELP WHEN I CAN. CAN'T WAIT TO MEET THE CREW.

Hannah sent a like and then tapped into the Lacy thread when a response came in, chuckling at the enthusiastic YES OF COURSE! I CAN'T WAIT!

"Looks like Lacy and Liam are both happy to help when they can." She slid her phone back into her pocket. "Lacy's farm provides all our eggs here at the restaurant, and we get other fresh produce and meats from local farms and ranches."

"Can't wait to see what you concoct for us," Kayla said.

Did Ryan's smile look a little forced? "Yeah. Can't wait."

Chapter Three

An hour and a half later, Hannah followed the cargo van the crew had rented, her gaze taking in the landscape as they turned down a road just outside of town limits that she'd never had cause to take before. "It's pretty out here," she said to Kayla, who'd opted for her passenger's seat instead of either the van Oran drove or the Jeep that Ryan, Trevor, and Lexi were in—filming, of course. Hannah wondered what narration he'd be giving as they wound their way through the countryside.

"I forget how much I miss green sometimes." Kayla rolled her window down and made a show of dragging in a long breath. "And spring in particular. Southern California just doesn't do spring like this."

"It's one of the things I missed most when I was out there." When the cargo van's turn signal flipped on, Hannah followed suit, though she couldn't see anything beyond the line of trees. "You grew up in Indiana, right?"

"That's right." Kayla sighed.

Hannah shot her a glance as she turned onto the long, winding driveway. "You sound a bit wistful. Missing home?"

Kayla shrugged. "Family more than anything else. I squeezed in a visit home last month, and my brothers and sister are each so settled, you know? House, spouse, two-point-five kids—the whole nine yards. I didn't think I wanted that. I mean, I get to travel the world and do what I love. But holding my baby niece just stirred up the yearning, I guess." She made a face. "And naturally, my mom was quick to point out that I'm not getting any younger. She offered to introduce me to three different men from her church who would be 'absolutely perfect' for me."

Hannah's smile felt a bit wistful too. "I get that. I wish my mom was here to participate in the prodding." She lifted her brows and dodged a deep pothole. "Did you meet any of these supposedly perfect guys?"

Kayla snorted. "Not of my own volition, but one of them just *happened* to show up at the restaurant we went to one night. Of course, my mom just happened to include an extra person in her reservation who couldn't make it after all, so we just happened to have an extra chair."

"What a coincidence," Hannah said, laughing as she pulled into a parking area beside the van. "I found myself in a similar situation when I moved home, thanks to a father and brother who 'just want to see me happy.' It's true, but their technique wasn't great."

"I know how that goes." Kayla shook her head, but amusement lit her eyes again. "And the guy was all right. But no sparks. Maybe I shouldn't be waiting for sparks though. Maybe that's the hopeless romantic in me."

Hannah unfastened her seat belt and shook her head. "You deserve sparks, Kayla. Don't settle for less. Though, to be fair, sometimes it takes more than one dinner for those sparks to ignite."

Also unbuckled, Kayla reached into the back seat for her tote bag. "Yeah, but when will I ever see him again? He's rooted in

Indiana. I mean, I wouldn't mind a husband and kids, but I'm not ready to give up everything I've worked for. I love my job. And—" She broke off, pressing her lips together.

Hannah lifted her brows. "And?"

Kayla was already opening the door. Avoiding the question, or just stepping into that job she so loved? Because a man strode from the door of the house, dressed in a crisp button-down shirt and pressed slacks.

He looked familiar enough that Hannah knew he must be a local, but she didn't know what name belonged with the face.

She wasn't left waiting for long. The man strode directly to Kayla with a hand extended and a smile. "Ford Payne," he said, shaking her hand. "You must be Kayla. I recognize you from your profile picture on the rental site."

Gone was the wistfulness of a moment before. Now Kayla was clearly in her professional persona, one that didn't reveal doubt about anything. Hannah quietly closed her car door as her friend shook hands with the owner of the rental house. She enjoyed seeing Kayla in her element like this.

"So good to meet you, Mr. Payne," Kayla said, beaming. "I can't thank you enough for giving us permission to film on your property. May I introduce you to the host of *Destination Discovery*?"

"It's Ford," he corrected her. "And yes, please do."

"And would you like to appear on camera? We love to include our local hosts wherever we go. It adds an element of authenticity to the show, and of course it could help drive traffic to your rentals. You have several in this area, don't you?"

Ford nodded. "Three. This house comes from my own family. We inherited another from my wife's parents, and we bought a third when the opportunity arose. Are you sure you'll have enough room in this one? We still have availability in the bungalow in town."

Kayla's smile didn't waver. "This is actually perfect for us, given that one of our camera operators is married to our sound engineer, so they only need one room. So what do you say about being in the show yourself?"

Ford gave an enthusiastic nod. "Of course, of course. I've seen the show, and I love how you incorporate so much local history into it."

Which was to say, he had known this was a possibility. Maybe that was why he was dressed in his Sunday best, right down to the shoes that looked like they came from somewhere fancier than a department store.

Kayla reached into the tote and pulled out a clipboard. "Awesome. I have a release here for you to sign, giving us permission to use your likeness on the show and in any promo clips we or the network choose to run on television or the internet. Please feel free to read it in its entirety and ask any questions you have. Then I'll introduce you to Ryan. We like to capture the first meeting on camera, if that's okay." She winked. "He's at his best when he's off-the-cuff and hearing things for the first time. Not that there aren't occasions when we need to do multiple takes, of course."

Ford took the clipboard with another nod. Rather than watch him read, Hannah wandered to the other side of the van to see what the rest of the crew was up to.

Lexi had massive earphones on, and she was fiddling with the soundboard strapped to her torso, the boom mic tucked under her arm and a frown between her brows. "Awfully windy," she muttered. Her gaze flicked to Ryan. "Mind grabbing the dead cat?"

Ryan nodded and strode to the van.

Hannah gaped. "The *what*?"

Lexi's frown dissolved into a smile. Ryan laughed and emerged a moment later with the shaggy cover that had been on the microphone at the restaurant. He brandished it with a wink to Hannah. "A little industry-naming humor. Because when it's lying discarded on the ground…" He held it flat, showing the mound of fur sticking out every which way.

Hannah laughed. "Gotcha. Though wouldn't *sleeping* cat sound a little nicer?"

Lexi took the thing from his outstretched hand. "No doubt. But we didn't name it. We just use it. You'll have to blame the old-timers for this one."

Trevor hoisted his massive camera onto his shoulder. Or maybe it wasn't the camera itself that was so massive. It was in some kind of harness.

Hannah tilted her head. "Will it be totally annoying if I ask you what other things are called? Like that harness on the camera?"

"As long as we're not in a take, ask whatever you want," Ryan assured her. "And that's a steadying harness, to keep the shot from looking shaky when we're on the move. On a feature, the cameras are often on dollies or tracks, but we don't have the budget for that. We make do with gyros and gimbals and harnesses."

Hannah nodded. "Feature?"

"A movie," Trevor clarified.

Oran jumped out of the van, a drone in hand. "There are lots of fun gadgets these days to make effects accessible even to little network shows like ours. I mean, back when I got started, we needed a jib—a kind of crane—for an aerial shot. These days, a drone does the trick."

Lexi snickered, and Oran shot her a playful glare.

Hannah looked between them. "What?"

Lexi laughed outright. "The drones can get a little pricey when you go through a gazillion of them when you're learning how to fly them."

Oran's cheeks went red, but he smiled too. "I only lost three."

"In the first month," Ryan stage-whispered.

"My favorite," Trevor put in, "was when we were in the Amazon and Oran pressed the 'return home' button. He didn't realize it was still set for *home*. As in, Los Angeles. Off it went, zooming northwest at top speed. It was out of range so fast he couldn't correct the error."

Oran sighed. "I still miss that drone. The shots I got with the backup weren't half as good, given the storm that moved in."

Ryan clapped a hand on Oran's shoulder. "He's an expert now though. Best drone pilot around."

"All right," Kayla called from where she still stood with Ford. "We're good. Ford, you go back up to the front door. Ryan, in the driver's seat of the Jeep."

The crew clearly knew their parts. As Ryan got behind the wheel, Oran set the drone aside and picked up his camera. He and Trevor took their places, one directly in front of Ryan, and the other off to the side.

Kayla came up beside Hannah and gave her elbow a little guiding tug. "Out of the shot," she said cheerfully. Once satisfied, she pulled a classic clapboard from her bag, wrote something on it with a dry-erase marker, and said, "Everyone come sync up your time codes."

Hannah watched as the three techs moved to the clapper, glanced at the digital clock readout, and adjusted their equipment.

Kayla smiled at Ford. "This allows us to keep filming even through mistakes. If we need to redo something, we'll interrupt and ask you to start over. With all our equipment synced, we can edit later with the time codes. So, take one, initial greeting." She clapped the top of the board, then jogged back to Hannah.

All was still for the count of five, and then Ryan burst from the Jeep, a huge smile on his face. "Wow, this place is gorgeous!" he proclaimed, as if he hadn't already gotten his first look at it. "And here's the owner of this beautiful rental, Ford Payne." As he spoke, he strode up the flagstone path toward the door, hand outstretched. "Ford, hello!"

Kayla leaned close to Hannah and whispered, "I prepped Ford to not look directly at the cameras, but let's see how he does. Nine times out of ten, we have to reshoot the greeting."

Ford, however, directed his beaming smile solely at Ryan and shook his hand. "Welcome to Blackberry Valley, Ryan."

"I'm excited to be here." Ryan glanced behind them at the house but faced the cameras and mic again before he spoke. "So how long has this house belonged to your family?"

"Oh, ever since it was built," Ford said. "Back in the 1850s. Used to be a farm, but most of the land was sold off in the early 1900s, after my great-great-grandfather died. He left everything to his wife and baby, but it was too much for her to keep up on her own, so she downsized. Her son, Judah—my great-grandfather—was the one who refurbished the house as you see it now, aside from some modernization my wife and I did." He motioned toward the flagstones. "The tour actually begins with this walkway. Grandpa Judah was a geologist who taught at a college in Lexington. Every stone you see here was one he collected for a specific purpose. These particular ones have fossils in them."

"Seriously?" Ryan stepped off the doorstep and back onto the path, crouching down to investigate. Oran came in to get a shot of whatever he was looking at. "No *way*! Is this a trilobite?"

Hannah's lips twitched at the catchphrase. She glanced over at Kayla, who was taking notes on a tablet.

"I believe so, yes," Ford answered.

Kayla called out, "Let's redo that."

Hannah followed her friend's gaze to see what was going on in time to see Ford wince. "Sorry, sorry. I looked at the camera."

"No problem. Happens all the time," Trevor said. "Count to five in your head and start over. Ryan just asked if that was a trilobite."

Hannah tuned them out as they talked for a minute about fossils—something she knew that Ryan, with his degree in archaeology, could never get enough of, though he tended to prefer human-made artifacts, if she recalled. She peered over Kayla's shoulder to see her taking notes of words and phrases from the conversation under a heading of *Things to Look Up.*

"For voiceover options," Kayla whispered to Hannah. "If I make notes now, I can be doing the research as we film, which means a quicker turnaround time once we get back to the studio. I also note the time stamp of obvious edits, like that redo."

"That makes sense," Hannah said. "Are you directing this too?"

Kayla made a so-so gesture with her hand. "Not in the way that a scripted show has a director, but sort of. I'm technically billed as a producer, as are Oran and Trevor. Any of us can call a cut or redo if we need it, but I'm usually the one with the slate. When we're on the move, I often have a camera—just as some of our guests have their own cameras that capture their individual perspectives. It helps us get as many angles on the scene as possible. But my primary role on the production is researcher."

"So your grandpa Judah—he's the son of Elinor Payne, correct?" Ryan's voice sounded a little different, regaining Hannah's attention. The cameras repositioned, which no doubt gave them a great view of the surprised frown on Ford's face.

"That's right," he said slowly.

Ryan couldn't be oblivious to his host's confusion—he was far too much of a people person and had great observational skills—but he barreled ahead. "Which makes you the great-great-great-nephew of Franklin Sullivan."

There was no mistaking it. Ford went stiff. "What do you mean? What does Franklin Sullivan have to do with anything?"

"Kayla?" Ryan called out.

Kayla pulled up a different tab on her tablet and scrolled furiously through what looked like a chain of emails. She paused, gaze flying across a few lines, and then glanced up again—not at Ryan, but at Ford. "In our email on March twentieth, I said we were researching the missing diamond known as the Crater of

Diamonds from a mine in Arkansas. It was allegedly stolen by Franklin Sullivan and hidden somewhere in Barren County in 1910. I asked if we could film here to further that research, and you agreed."

Ford swallowed. "I must have skimmed over the part about Sullivan. Sorry, just took me by surprise. My wife's always accusing me of not reading things carefully." He gave them a sheepish smile. "She usually handles all the reservations for that very reason, but I was so excited to have you that she let me take over the correspondence."

Kayla's shoulders relaxed. "Is it okay to talk to you about Franklin Sullivan then? He's a big part of the story, so we can't ignore him."

"Of course, of course." Ford waved the concern away and gave his shoulders a roll, presumably to loosen them. "Sorry about that. Can we pick it back up?"

"Sure." Ryan put his TV smile on again, waited a few seconds, and then restated his question about Franklin Sullivan.

This time Ford managed to smile. "That's right. He's the legendary black sheep of the family. Brother of Judah's mother, Elinor. She came from Chicago."

Ryan nodded along. "So the story is that Franklin Sullivan, Elinor's brother, got involved with unsavory company. I've seen speculation about whether it was Chicago's Irish Mafia, or anarchists."

Ford shrugged. "I've seen the same speculation. Maybe one or the other, maybe both. We don't know for sure. According to family stories, though, he put Elinor in quite a pickle when he showed up with the law on his tail."

"And the diamond in hand—or so the story goes." Ryan waved his arm toward the fields surrounding the house. "So what do you think? Did he stash the diamond somewhere around here?"

Ford's shrug seemed more at ease now, as did his smile. "That's the story. And I can tell you, my siblings and I spent many a summer day hunting in every groundhog hole and under every tree root for it."

Ryan swung back to Ford with a grin. "I'm guessing you didn't find it, or we wouldn't be here."

Ford held up a finger. "Not *yet*, Ryan. That's the key word. We haven't found it *yet*."

Ryan faced the camera. He was apparently allowed to, though the guests were supposed to focus on him. "I like this guy. Not *yet*. Well, let's see if we can turn that 'not yet' into a 'eureka,' shall we?"

"And cut," Kayla called. "You were awesome, Ford. A natural."

Ford laughed. "No need for flattery. But I appreciate you giving me a chance to try again. Now." He clapped his hands together and motioned to the house. "How about I show you folks around?"

Chapter Four

Elinor Payne finished the last stitch in the patch she was sewing onto the knee of Judah's trousers and snipped off the thread. The other knee already had a patch on it, so at least now they matched. One more tumble as her fearless little boy went exploring, and she'd have to give in and make him a new pair.

She smoothed a hand over the patch, remembering the joy on his face when he had come in for dinner, covered in dirt from head to toe and holding up a rock like he'd found a hidden treasure. She smiled now as she did then, as she could never help doing when Judah showed her one of his discoveries.

To her eye, they rarely looked like anything special. She could see the allure when they had the impressions of ancient creatures in them, or when he cracked open one of the geodes his uncle sent him so often. But often it was the pattern, shape, or color of the rock itself that caught his eye.

What lessons he taught her every day. To look for beauty in the mundane. To count as precious every facet of the world God had made.

She set down her mending and cast a glance out the window, where she could see the glow of the moon. These quiet evening hours breathed peace and contentment over her soul. Sometimes, though, she couldn't help but glance at the chair beside the fireplace and miss the man who had once occupied it. Miss evenings spent in conversation, not quiet solitude.

Tom had been gone for four years now. The ache had lessened, but it never went away. How could it, when she saw him smiling at her from their son's face every day? When she heard Tom's quick wit from Judah's mouth, or saw his intrigue with the natural world through the little boy's bright eyes?

She reached for the newspaper she had yet to open today. The article on the front page about the bill up for debate in the senate made her mind drift back to that year she spent in the capital. To the day she finally convinced her aunt to go with her to the Smithsonian Museum. To the man who caught her attention because his was so firmly focused on a dinosaur skeleton.

She'd never seen anyone so transfixed. Certainly, she also felt some awe over the enormous creature and had read the placard to learn more about it. But the handsome young man studied it as if he were cataloguing each bone.

Her lips tugged up at the memory. Her curiosity tended more toward people and their behavior than art or artifacts. And so, much to the horror of her old-fashioned aunt, she sidled up to him and struck up a conversation, asking him what he knew about the prehistoric animal. How he knew it. What had brought him to DC when his accent clearly branded him as a Southerner, as surely as her own made it clear she was from Chicago.

They ended up touring the rest of the museum together, his intelligence even winning Aunt Coraline over. Elinor learned he had recently completed his studies in biology and would be spending the summer in DC before going back to his family farm in Kentucky to take over operations.

By the time he left the capital three months later, they were married. She came with him to this Kentucky home and made it her own. She was welcomed by his family, despite a few grumbles about his bringing home a Yankee, and settled into a life she never dreamed she'd take to so easily.

Elinor, a farmer's wife. She, who had spent her entire twenty-two years in big cities up until then. She, who had gone to school to study literature because she craved an education. Oh, how her family had laughed when she had gone home to introduce Tom and announced that she'd be moving south and helping him take over the farm.

Blinking, Elinor tried to push the memories away. Usually, she was able to these days. Judah kept her busy, as did the book reviews she wrote for the newspaper in Lexington. But today was the anniversary of that first time she met Tom, a date they always celebrated along with their wedding anniversary.

Eight years since they'd met. But she'd been alone for half of those. The years since his death would soon outnumber the ones they'd had together. A bit of melancholy was understandable.

"Focus on the joy, Elinor," she murmured to herself. As she taught Judah to do at the end of every day. Count the blessings instead of the woes. Count the joy instead of the tears. And there were plenty of blessings, plenty of joys. She wouldn't trade this life for anything—in this town that had become home, with the neighbors and family who had claimed her as their own, in this place Tom had left for her and Judah.

She skimmed the front page of the paper, but her mind wasn't on legislation or its repercussions. Her gaze drifted to the window again. This would be the first planting season since she sold off the farmland, and she still worried that Tom wouldn't approve. He had wanted to preserve the family legacy for Judah.

But it had been too much for her to keep up with. She'd made a fine farmer's wife when it had meant cooking and making their clothes and keeping the house. She even tended the chickens with a smile. But tilling the land went far beyond her skill set. After Tom died, she accepted the neighbors' offer to rent the fields from her, and then when they offered to buy all but the five acres surrounding the house and reaching down to the tree line, she agreed once more.

The money she put away from the sale would cover Judah's education someday and helped support them now too. She still had her chickens, and she sold most of the eggs. She made a bit from her book reviews, and she started a shift at the library last winter. When Judah began school next autumn, she would pick up more hours. Between that and the piano lessons she gave, it was enough.

She turned the page in the newspaper, and the headline on the left side caught her eye. CHICAGO CRIMINAL ON THE LOOSE IN THE SOUTH.

Anything having to do with Chicago always piqued her interest, so she set aside thoughts of Tom and read the first paragraph.

It was all she could manage. Her eyes stuck on the name given in those first lines and refused to go any farther. *Franklin Sullivan.*

No, it wasn't the appearance of her brother's name in an article about criminals that stopped her—he'd appeared in plenty, given his decade on Chicago's police force. It was the fact that this article claimed *he* was the criminal on the loose in the South.

"Ridiculous." She read through the rest of the article, thinking there must have been a mistake in that opening line, or perhaps it was another Franklin Sullivan. There were surely several in Chicago, as common as her maiden name was.

But no. It clearly stated that her brother, a former law enforcement officer, was a known collaborator of the Ragen's Colts Irish Mafia and had association with several of the Chicago Anarchists. Her chest felt so tight she could scarcely continue.

Franklin wasn't much for letter-writing, but he sent gifts for Judah so frequently she accused him of spoiling the boy. She hadn't seen him since Christmas, but that had only been a few months ago. He couldn't have fallen so far so fast. Could he?

The newspaper drifted down, her eyes going unfocused. It had to be a mistake. Franklin had been her rock when they were growing up, her hero. He'd always been the sort to defend the defenseless, to put a halt to fistfights, to give up his lunch to someone who was hungry. The thought that he could have turned crooked, eventually abandoning his position to lead a life of crime? And that her father's only response when questioned was, "No comment"?

It made no sense. None.

And why hadn't her parents sent her a telegram, if Franklin was really being hunted by the law—and if he was somewhere in the South?

That made as little sense as the accusation itself. She went back to the newspaper, her jaw dropping at the words she read. According to the article, one of Franklin's associates had a brother in Arkansas who had come into possession of the largest diamond ever pulled from a four-year-old mine in the town of Kimberly. And Franklin had stolen that diamond and was now on the run.

She dropped the paper again, scowling at it. This couldn't be her brother. Franklin had never been motivated by greed. He'd always been perfectly content to be a public servant.

Although...last year hadn't he cited his financial situation as the reason he'd yet to marry and start a family? He'd said that between the risk of his job and the modest pay that came with it, he didn't feel he had anything to offer a woman.

What if he'd met someone and fallen in love? What if that someone wanted more than a police officer's salary? Would that be enough to tempt her brother off the straight and narrow?

Something creaked from the direction of the kitchen. She sprang to her feet, pulse racing, then scolded herself. Just the wind tugging on the screen door, most likely. Judah couldn't reach the latch on the door, and she forgot to check half the time after he came in for the evening.

Yet there was no other sign of strong winds. No whistling through the eaves, no skittering of last year's fallen leaves, nor rustling of the new ones. No tones from the wind chimes Tom had hung for her on the back porch when they first moved in.

And there—another creak, this one sounding suspiciously like the floorboard beside the table.

There was no doubt about it. Someone was in her house. And while neighbors often let themselves in, they didn't do it sneakily. They called out a greeting or knocked as they entered. And rarely at all after dark.

When they first moved in, Tom kept a hunting rifle over the mantel. She'd insisted he move it, not liking it to be the primary focus of the room. She was suddenly glad that he'd built a case for it and kept it here in the main room. She opened the case now and drew out the rifle, raising it to her shoulder as she moved silently toward the hallway that connected to the kitchen.

The rifle wasn't loaded, and she'd only fired it once—enough to know she didn't want it kicking her in the shoulder ever again—but whoever was in her kitchen didn't need to know that. And she had the benefit of knowing each noisy board in her house. The intruder certainly didn't. Otherwise, they'd have avoided that second squeak by the sink.

Glad she always left a lamp burning in there until she went to bed, she quickly strode into the hallway, three steps to the kitchen, and swung her harmless rifle toward the sink.

A man reached for the lamp, but before he could extinguish it, she caught a glimpse of his face.

Her rifle sagged a bit. "Franklin?"

Her brother spun, hand falling away from the oil lamp. When he saw her—or perhaps her gun—his eyes went wide and his hands shot up. "Ellie, don't shoot. It's me."

She lowered the weapon with a huff. "I couldn't if I wanted to. It's not loaded."

Franklin frowned. "You confronted an intruder with an unloaded weapon? Haven't I taught you anything?"

He was going to chide *her*? She switched her hold, raising it like a bat. "I can always club you. Maybe I will, if you don't make quick work of telling me why the Lexington paper has an article about how you're an outlaw."

He winced and moved one of his raised hands to swipe off the hat that had seen better days. His hair was far longer than usual, ragged and oily. "I was hoping that wouldn't make it all the way down here."

"Well, it did." She pointed with the rifle toward the table and chairs. "Sit. Talk. Now."

He pulled out a chair, and the way he sagged into it made her aware of the lines of exhaustion on his face, the layer of dust on his clothes, the slight shake in his hand. "I don't know what that article says, but it isn't the truth, I can promise you that."

"No? You didn't steal a diamond from someone in Arkansas?" She didn't mean for it to come out like an accusation.

But if he wasn't on the run from the law, what was he doing here?

The way he screwed up his face did nothing to assuage her fears. "All right, it can't have the reasons straight. I'm not a crook, El—"

"Did you or did you not steal a diamond?" Her words came out higher pitched than she intended, but at least she kept her volume low. Given the too-curious little boy asleep right above them, that was something.

"Well, yes, but—"

She dropped the rifle onto the table so that she could brace herself on the chair opposite him. Just now, she needed the support. Her gaze stayed fastened to the face she would have known anywhere yet wasn't sure she recognized.

Her brother had never looked so forlorn. So desperate. So weary.

What had he gotten himself into?

He heaved a long breath and rubbed a dirty hand over his equally dirty face. "I didn't know where else to go. But no one will think to look for me here, to connect me to you. I was hoping I could rest for a day or two."

Her fingers went tight on the rungs of the chair. "Franklin, I have a child. If you're on the run from the law, you can't expect—"

"I would never endanger Judah. Or you, for that matter." He seemed both sincere and hurt that she would question it. He laid his hands on the table, palms up. "I promise you, it's not what you think. I need you to trust me. I can't tell you everything, because it could endanger you if you knew, but I need you to believe I'm not a criminal."

Not a criminal, but he admitted to theft? She shook her head in confusion. He sounded like the brother she'd always known, loved, and looked up to. He wore the same expression as when he'd made her promise, before she went off to school, that she'd use the skills he taught her to defend herself if anyone ever tried to hurt her.

But he obviously had dangerous secrets.

She held his gaze a moment more and then drew in a breath. "Are you hungry?"

His shoulders sagged. "Starving. Thanks, Ellie."

"Don't thank me yet." She turned to the pantry, mentally sifting through the offerings for something quick but filling. "You can't stay in the house if someone's after you. I'm sorry, Franklin, but my priority is Judah's safety. I can't let anyone bring danger to him. Not even you."

"I know. I wasn't going to ask."

She motioned to the sink. "Get yourself cleaned up while I make you a sandwich."

She heard him pumping the water while she gathered the bread she'd baked that morning, a wheel of cheese, and then fished the leftover roast from the icebox. He used the sliver of soap to wash up while she sliced the cheese, and then he leaned against the counter, watching her.

"I know I can't risk bringing any attention to you and Judah. But I thought maybe you'd know where to point me. Somewhere nearby that no one would think to look?"

Her brows knit, but nothing sprang to mind. But then, she'd never been the one who was good in a crisis. "I don't know. I'll give it some thought." She offered him the plated sandwich along with a frown. "You could stay in the cellar for tonight. It's too dark to find your way to anything else anyway."

He opened his mouth as if to argue, then apparently changed his mind. "If I wasn't about to collapse from exhaustion, I'd refuse. But only one night. I won't bring trouble to your door."

He really did seem to be on the verge of collapse. His movements were sluggish, and he swayed a little. She poured a glass of milk for him and nudged him back to the chair. "Sit before you fall over. I'll grab some spare blankets and a pillow."

"Don't go to any trouble," he said around a mouthful of sandwich. "I've been sleeping without such luxuries for weeks."

"Weeks?" But she raised a hand when she saw from his face that he hadn't meant to say even that much. "No, that's fine. I don't want to know." She did, of course. But if the law came looking for him, she'd rather not have anything to tell them. "But you'll have a pillow and some blankets, and that's that."

She bustled off to fetch them while he ate, though once out of sight, she paused. Leaned against the wall, let her eyes slide shut. Tried to pray, though she didn't know what to say beyond, *Lord, please...*

How often had she wished she could see her brother more? They were close when they were young, closer than any of her friends were with their brothers. He was always there to protect her, to teach her, to encourage her. He'd been her champion, her hero, her friend. When he and Tom hit it off at once, she knew she'd made the right decision in accepting Tom's proposal.

They tried to lure Franklin to Blackberry Valley, promising a quiet life even if he stayed in law enforcement, but Franklin had laughed and said he didn't want a quiet life. He wanted to keep fighting for right, for justice. Protecting the innocent in the places that seemed so bent on harming them.

That couldn't have changed. Could it?

She shook herself and padded quietly up the stairs to the linen closet, knowing her soft steps wouldn't wake Judah. He always slept through her comings and goings after she put him to bed. The little bit of light reaching up from the ground floor was enough to illuminate the hallway and the knob she turned. She grabbed a couple of old quilts and a spare pillow.

She hated to think of her brother sleeping in the cold, damp cellar, but it would be better than outdoors, especially if rain moved in overnight as the clouds on the horizon at dusk had indicated. In fact, she heard the first patter of drops on the roof, and the moonlight had vanished.

Definitely not a good night for Franklin to be wandering any farther. And hopefully, if anyone followed him, the rain would hide his tracks and inspire them to take shelter somewhere too.

She closed the linen closet, shaking her head at herself. Was she really hoping her brother could escape the law? Did that make her a criminal too?

Her fingers dug into the fabric, soft from years of washing. She couldn't think that way. She would choose to believe her brother. He had never once lied to her. Never once shown himself to be anything but the best of men.

She'd give him the benefit of the doubt. She'd assume he had his reasons, good ones, even if he wouldn't tell her what they were.

And if the law shows up looking for him? a voice in her head asked. *Will you lie to protect him?*

That was a question she wasn't sure how to answer, given the lack of information at war with her deep-seated belief in Franklin. So for now, she shoved it aside and moved quietly back down the stairs, into the kitchen.

Her brother had finished the sandwich and appeared about to fall asleep in his chair. He perked up a bit when she came into the room, arms full of linens. He pushed to his feet. "Thanks, Sis."

She pressed the bedding into his arms and stood on tiptoe to kiss his cheek. "You've always watched out for me," she said softly. "How could I do any less for you?"

He met her gaze, and through his exhaustion, through his worry, she saw that familiar gleam—the one that said he was a man worth emulating, one who loved God and his neighbor, who would do anything for anyone who needed it.

And if she was wrong? She drew back, folding her arms over her middle and willing a smile to her lips. "You remember where the cellar door is?"

He moved toward the door to the porch. He'd have to walk around to the south-facing side of the house to find the low entrance to the cellar. They didn't have a way to get to it that didn't involve going outside, which was a mighty inconvenience in the winter or the rain.

"Come back in the morning," she said as he pushed the screen door open. "I'll have breakfast for you, and some food to take with you. I'll think of someplace to send you by then. Where you'll be safe."

He nodded but didn't step outside. Maybe he was hesitant to dash through the rain, or maybe he didn't want to leave quite yet. "What time does Judah usually get up? I'll try to avoid him. I don't want to put him in an awkward spot."

Her smile went genuine. "He's not the early riser you've always been. He doesn't usually come down until eight or so."

Franklin offered a tired, sad smile. "I'm sorry, Ellie. I am. But even so...it's good to see you."

He spared her the need to respond by slipping out into the night.

Elinor sank into the chair he'd left and wondered what in the world she was going to do.

Chapter Five

Hannah slipped into the house with Kayla behind the film crew, her jaw dropping even as she registered Ryan's exclamations of surprise and appreciation from whatever room Ford had led him into.

She could have echoed his every "No *way!*" Everywhere she looked was something beautiful and unexpected, from the geodes built into the stair risers to the rainbow of rocks plastered into the wall along the hallway instead of a chair rail. She turned wide eyes on Kayla. "I had no idea there was a house like this in Blackberry Valley. Or anywhere for that matter."

"Cool, huh?" Kayla closed the front door behind them and motioned her into what appeared to be a large living room. "I looked up the house for the show, and when I saw it was listed as a short-term vacation rental, I was already excited. Then when I saw the pictures, I was downright giddy."

"Giddy sums up my reaction to this kitchen too," Hannah said as she stepped into it, eyes wide. She admitted that, given Ford's claims that his great-grandfather had been the one to make most of the updates to the house, she'd expected it to be old-fashioned and outdated. But this was a farmhouse-style kitchen worthy of the magazines, with a huge central island, copper pots dangling from a ceiling-mounted rack, wide windows letting golden sunlight stream in, and acres of counter space.

"Suitable for your needs?" Kayla asked with a laugh.

Hannah snorted. "It'll do, I guess." She ran her hand along the smooth granite counter—white, with veins of blue and copper. "Wow."

"I know you haven't had time to make plans yet, but let me know how you'd like to handle buying supplies and groceries. I can either come shopping with you and use my card, or you can take care of everything and then invoice us." Kayla swung her tote bag onto the big wooden table. "I figured we'd eat at the Hot Spot tonight, but do you think you could have something together in time that we could do breakfast here? I know Ryan will be eager to scout the area and will want to get an early start."

Hannah opened cabinets and drawers to take stock of the equipment. Most of them were empty. There were plenty of plates and bowls, flatware and glasses, but only the minimum when it came to pots and pans—the pretty set hanging above the island. "I'll have to bring some of my own equipment, for sure," she said. "Maybe borrow a few things from the restaurant or prep some stuff there and transport it." At least the fridge was enormous. That would help. "As for the food itself, I'm planning to get it from my usual wholesale suppliers and then invoice you. Breakfast tomorrow shouldn't be a problem."

She was already mentally adding to her usual orders as menu options churned through her imagination. Perhaps she could source pastries from Sweet Caroline's Bakery or Jump Start Coffee, owned by Jacob's brother, Zane. That would free up her time to focus on the other meals, and pastries were great for the always-available table.

And maybe a charcuterie board to include some savory options. She'd still have to do a grocery run for things they didn't carry at the Hot Spot, like individually wrapped bars, crackers, chips, and yogurts, but that wouldn't be too bad.

This was going to be so much fun. "Does anyone have any food allergies or preferences I need to know about?"

Kayla shook her head. "Not with this bunch. We have a much bigger crew on our more elaborate trips, and some of them have special dietary needs, but this group will eat anything."

Hannah considered pulling out her phone to take notes, but she preferred to see everything at a glance and not to have to scroll constantly. "I don't suppose you have paper and a pen in that magic bag of yours, do you? I need to start making a list."

"Never go anywhere without them." Kayla handed over a memo pad and pen. "There's plenty more where that came from, if you need it." She motioned to the door. "I'm going to peek in on the others. If you need me, you know where to find me."

"Yep, thanks." Though she could still hear the murmur of voices, Hannah had no trouble tuning them out as she pulled a stool from under the island and got to work. First, ideas for the various meals. Kayla had said they'd be there for ten days, so thirty meals. Well, Hannah would need a day off at some point, so she'd talk to Kayla about another night eating out—breakfast and lunch would be easy to prepare in advance. In fact, they might want to schedule a few meals out, to get a taste for what Blackberry Valley had to offer. She'd check on that but assume it would be more like twenty-five to twenty-seven meals.

The voices grew louder, Ford's rising above the others as they came toward the kitchen. "And here we have my wife's favorite room in the whole house," he said, stepping in and greeting Hannah with a nod. "This room is actually an addition from the 1940s. The original kitchen was probably pretty small. Then Denise updated the appliances and countertops a few years ago."

"It's gorgeous," Hannah said, eyes drifting to the counter again. "I love this granite."

Ford grinned. "We do too—so much so that we redid our own kitchen with it. And of course, Grandpa Judah's love of geology is in here too, like every other room in the house." He motioned to the entrance.

It took Hannah a moment to realize that the doorframes weren't simple wood. Rocks and stones surrounded them. It looked so natural and organic, she hadn't even noticed them at first.

The other members of the crew crowded in so they could see.

"You'll find the same kind of thing in each of the bedrooms," Ford explained. "The whole house is a testament to Grandpa Judah's work."

"Dude, you're going to be overwhelmed with reservations after this episode airs." Trevor pointed his camera toward the doorframe and did a slow rotation.

The crew scurried out of the way but didn't stop chattering. Hannah moved to Kayla's side, brows drawn. "Do we need to be quiet?"

"Nah, he's just getting some B-roll." At Hannah's blank look, she grinned. "All the filler shots that are used to establish a scene or during narration, often in a sort of montage. We'll probably cut together some shots of the geology used in the house while Ryan says something clever and witty about it."

"Like 'This house rocks,'" Ryan said with a wink.

Kayla rolled her eyes. "Or maybe I'll write him something."

"How about 'We couldn't wait to *dig up* clues in this house'? Or 'We knew we could take nothing for *granite*'?" Ryan elbowed Hannah. "Get it?"

Hannah shook her head. "Good to see you haven't changed, Ryan. You still love your puns."

Oran slid up on Ryan's other side, his camera doing a sweep too. "I got him a shirt for Christmas that says, 'Intend your puns, you coward!'"

Ford checked his watch. "Well, folks, I have to run. Anything else I can do for you this afternoon?"

Kayla stepped forward. "I think we're good for now, but we would really appreciate it if you could poke around in your family history and pass along anything you find out about Franklin Sullivan."

Their host nodded. "Will do." He hesitated, then said, "Don't be surprised if you hear from my daughter, Brooke. But don't feel like you have to indulge her in any way."

Ryan shot a look toward Kayla but then refreshed his smile for their host. "Noted." He reached out to shake Ford's hand again. "And we can't thank you enough for having us, Ford, and for letting us film here. I promise you won't regret it. We might tell a story about your infamous ancestor, but we'll be respectful."

Ford's smile went a little crooked, but it didn't falter. "Guess it's trendy these days to have an outlaw in the family. And if you need anything at all, don't hesitate to reach out. Kayla has my cell phone number." Ford looked at Hannah. "Glad to know Denise's beautiful work will be put to good use. You feel free to text if you need any-thing too, Hannah. We love your restaurant."

That never got old. "Thanks so much, Ford. Please tell Denise this kitchen is a dream and I'm excited to work in it over the next ten days."

Farewells were exchanged, and Ford let himself out of the house.

Ryan clapped twice and pointed to the island. Oran, Trevor, and Lexi set their gear down and pulled out stools. Kayla slid onto one on Hannah's left side, leaving one stool open.

Ryan, however, moved to the opposite side of the island to face them, his film-ready grin relaxing into an expression Hannah could only define as businesslike. "Okay, guys," he said, his voice calmer than it ever was on camera. "We need to take this afternoon and evening to develop our plan, since we didn't have time to do it before we left LA. After you've gotten your fill of B-roll and wild tracks, check in with Kayla for research assignments and planning."

Hannah leaned close to her friend. "Okay, you explained B-roll, but what are wild tracks?"

"Think B-roll for audio," Kayla replied in a whisper. "Ambient noises, room tone, bird calls, wind through the trees. That sort of thing."

"Ah. Thanks." Hannah was quickly discovering all she didn't know about the film business. After living so long in Los Angeles, she thought she'd picked up a lot. But she'd never really been involved in a production before. Even when she helped with craft services those couple of times, she had little to no interaction with the crew, other than when they came to the table and the conversa-tions had revolved around food. And though Oran had almost always had a camera with him when they'd hung out as a group all those years ago, it had just been for fun, so there was no shop talk.

"We'll do any research we can tonight so Kayla can get call sheets ready for the first couple of days, at least. Kayla, don't stress about getting those for the whole shoot yet. We're probably going to have to improvise a lot. See what we can find from local sources and pivot as necessary. The reenactment portion will have to wait until we know the story in full—if necessary, we'll fake it in the studio." Ryan's grin flashed. "Sorry. I know you hate that."

Kayla heaved an exaggerated sigh. "I'm the one who threw this one into the schedule, so if I complain, just remind me of that." She winked at Hannah. "Call sheets are the production schedules for each day that tell everyone where to show up and when and with what equipment. So, for instance, Oran knows when to have the drone out versus his main camera, when we need to have any locals on-site, and how long we can spend in each location."

"I think we've told you before that we rarely film in the same order a show appears in, right?" Ryan asked. When Hannah nodded, he went on. "The call sheets are how we organize our time most efficiently, so we're filming scenes in places that are close together all at once, rather than hauling gear back and forth and back again."

"And usually," Kayla added, leaning onto the island and reaching for her tote, "I've already organized our schedule before we come. This is going to be way more freewheeling than I like."

"Kayla's our resident organizational freak of nature," Lexi said with a grin.

"And that's why we can't live without her," Ryan added. "Any additional instructions, Kayla?"

Kayla had a memo pad from her tote. She flipped through a few pages and shook her head. "No, but we'll need to have a meeting tomorrow morning to finalize plans. Maybe during breakfast, or right after?"

"During. Better use of time. Let's say eight?"

Kayla scrolled on her phone. "Might as well make it nine. The forecast is calling for showers in the early morning, so that'll give them time to clear out. I'll have research assignments ready for everyone in an hour. I'll need whatever you've found back by eight tonight so I can at least get tomorrow's call sheet done."

Hannah stared at her friend as she talked. It wasn't so different, in some ways, from running a kitchen—knowing what was coming in when, which staff was available, and what equipment there was to work with. But she'd never seen Kayla in her element like this, to realize she played the role of head chef, but with a production crew instead of sous-chefs and servers.

Ryan's gaze moved to Hannah. "Anything you need from us, Hannah?"

"I figured I'd chat with you and Kayla about the number of meals to be served here versus times you might want to go out to try the local restaurants, but that's it. Otherwise, I'll just do a quick inventory of what's here and what I need to bring, then I'll head back to the Hot Spot and draw up my plan."

Kayla tapped something into her tablet. "Sounds good. Maybe we could also run some of our questions about the area by you? I figure even if you don't know the answers, you'll have a better idea of where to go with those questions than we would."

"Of course. Lacy and her husband will be a great resource for that too. Neil owns the local bookstore and has a thing for maps, so he knows a lot about the region. And Liam's been pretty much everywhere in the county thanks to his duties. Do you need me to come back out tonight?"

"No, tomorrow should be fine." Kayla looked up from her tablet with a smile. "I can always text you with anything that can't wait. Mostly, you just focus tonight on doing what you do best and decide what to feed us."

"Most important thing right there," Trevor agreed with a laugh.

Lexi reached over to pat her husband's flat belly. "Fair warning, this one's a bottomless pit."

"And never gains an ounce," Oran grumbled. "It's not fair."

"All right." Ryan clapped again. "Everyone get to it. Keep an eye on your emails for your instructions from Kayla and meet back here at six. We'll head to the Hot Spot for dinner then."

The crew slid off their stools, reclaimed their gear, and left the room, chattering about what to film and record. Kayla was doing something with her tablet again, and Ryan leaned against the counter. "So how many must-try restaurants are around here, other than yours?" he asked Hannah.

"Quite a few, depending on what you're in the mood for. I'll make a list." She jotted a note to herself to text Zane about pastries—or maybe she'd stop by when she got back into town. Then she glanced over at Kayla. "And how about I make a list of the people around town who are up on local history? I've run into quite a few of them since moving home."

Kayla slung an arm around Hannah's neck, nearly pulling her off her stool. "You're the absolute best."

Figuring she might as well get to her feet anyway so she could record a more thorough inventory, she chuckled and hugged Kayla back. "Hey, I'm just glad you guys found an excuse to visit. It's been way too long."

"On that, we can all agree." Ryan drew in a long breath, his smile going soft as he looked at the two of them. "Sometimes I miss the old days, you know? When no one recognized us, we had no budget, and everything was an adventure. I mean, we've worked hard to get here, and I'm grateful. But it's different now."

"By recognized *us*, he means people now recognize *him*," Kayla told Hannah. "Some of us can still walk around in public without anyone looking twice."

"By which she means *she* can," Ryan returned in a matching tone. He waved a hand toward the doorway. "The crew always gets attention, what with all their gear. Kayla's the only one who can get anything done without drawing a crowd of curious onlookers."

"Just call me the ghost." Kayla wiggled her fingers at them with a spooky wail.

"All right, ghost and clown," Hannah said. "Clear out of my kitchen and let me get to work. Kayla, I'll find you before I leave."

"Great." Kayla scooped her stuff off the island and put it all back in her tote. "I'm going to go claim a bedroom while the others are out and get my laptops set up."

Hannah blinked after her friend as Kayla strode from the room. "Did she say *laptops*? Plural?"

Ryan's gaze was still on the door Kayla had passed through. "She travels with five different monitors too. Well, not that they're all for her, to be fair. We set up a mobile studio wherever we go so we can review footage on-site and rerecord anything we need to. It's called a video village."

Hannah, paper and pen in hand, moved to the cabinets closest to the door. "This is going to be so much fun, learning the behind-the-scenes of what you guys do."

"Fair warning—it's not all glamorous." Ryan finally looked from the empty doorway to her. "But I bet you know all about that, huh? I guess making a fancy meal is about washing dishes and chopping onions as much as it is that final presentation."

Exactly. But just to make him laugh, she lifted her nose and gave a condescending sniff. "I don't know what you're talking about. I have *people* for that."

Ryan did indeed chuckle his way toward the exit. "Lucky you. Well, I don't, so I'd better get to work." But he paused halfway through the threshold and leaned back in to grin at her. "Glad Kayla found this, Hannah. We've missed you. I mean, I know we hadn't gotten together in years, even before you moved home. But somehow it was different, always knowing we could. Funny, isn't it? How we don't always realize how much people mean to us until they're no longer where we expect them to be?"

A feeling Hannah knew well, especially after her mother's death. "Yeah. A good reminder to tend our relationships. I'm glad you guys came too."

One more smile and he disappeared, leaving Hannah to make her lists in peace.

First, though, she finally opened the text from Marshall.

Hi, Hannah. Can you help me plan a surprise for Raquel? The six-month anniversary of our first date is coming up, and even though I can't be there, I want to do something special. Would you maybe have time to help plant some gifts around town for me? I have a plan for a special dinner too. Jacob's already in on it. Raquel just texted me that you're busy helping with a tv show or something, so if this is too much, I'll see if Elaine can help instead. I'm hoping to have everything happen on Monday so we can use the restaurant while it's closed, if that's ok? Jacob suggested that.

Hannah's thumbs flew to type her response. I'd love to help you surprise Raquel. Just let me know what you need me to do, and of course it's okay to use the restaurant.

And how sweet was it that Marshall was going to so much trouble for a half-year anniversary? Clearly he was going the second mile to make his relationship with Raquel work long-distance, despite some of the troubles they'd had since he moved to Chicago for a job. It was good to see.

A smile on her lips, Hannah got down to business.

Chapter Six

Hannah handed the smaller box to Lacy, grabbed the last one for herself, and balanced it on her hip so she could close the hatch of her Subaru Outback. "Last haul," she said, slipping her car key into her pocket and repositioning the box in her arms.

Lacy led the way back toward the kitchen entrance they'd been going in and out of. The morning rain had slowed to a drizzle, so they hadn't bothered with rain gear—though they both gave their boots a good wipe on the rug inside the mudroom door. "Awesome. The smell of those pastries is driving me crazy. We're allowed to eat too, right?"

"Testing all the food is the responsibility of a chef." Hannah inhaled the yeasty-sweet smell of the cinnamon rolls in the oven and the coffee Zane had provided. They'd agreed that she'd pick up the trays of goodies before they were baked and do that on-site so they'd be fresh and warm.

"How long until they're done?" Lacy slid her box onto the island and went to peer into the oven.

Hannah checked the timer on her watch. "Two minutes. Want to grab the icing out of the fridge while I put stuff away?"

"Sure."

Humming one of the Easter hymns they'd sung in church on Sunday, Hannah moved to the first boxes they'd brought in and began unpacking them, stowing each piece of equipment and the ingredients in empty cabinets.

"You're really putting your stuff *away*-away? Aren't you afraid you'll leave something here?" Lacy asked.

Hannah glanced over her shoulder at her friend, who'd pulled a drawer open and fished out a knife. "There's too much to leave it all out on the counters. An organized kitchen is an efficient kitchen. But don't worry. I made a list of everything I brought with me, and I'll check it all off as I repack. Plus, I already decided I wouldn't mix my stuff with the house's stuff in any of the cabinets or drawers. There are enough empty ones that I can keep it all separated."

"Smart." Lacy took the knife and icing over to the counter adjacent to the oven. "Now, which of these has the oven mitts?"

"Drawer on the other side of the oven." She'd also already written down what was stored where, for easy reference. "How are the rolls looking?" Even as she asked, her watch's alarm sounded.

Lacy tugged on the mitts and then opened the oven a crack. A smile bloomed on her face. "Golden brown and mouthwatering." She lowered the door the rest of the way and soon had the two pans out and sitting on the stovetop.

Hannah came over for a peek. "Mm. I'm getting hungry. You want to handle the icing?"

"I'm on it."

Hannah went back to work, grateful that Lacy had called in some extra help at the farm so that she could be there with Hannah from eight to two every day. And Liam was on first shift at the firehouse for the next few days, so he planned to come out each evening to help with dinner and cleanup, other than when the crew would be going out.

Of course, this was assuming that Jacob, Elaine, Raquel, and Dylan could handle everything at the restaurant and she wasn't called in for anything.

This was a good test for each of them, to see how the team did when she stepped back for a few days…and how she did in a kitchen without them. Lacy and Liam were both more than competent, of course, but neither were trained chefs.

By the end of this production, she and her employees would probably be very happy to see one another again, but also hopefully confident in their skills.

"Has anyone seen the key to the cargo van?" The voice was masculine, but it filtered into the kitchen through several layers of house, so Hannah wasn't entirely certain if it was Oran or Trevor.

"Bowl on the entryway table." That was Ryan.

"No, it's not." This time the voice was closer, and she recognized it as Oran's.

Ryan's steps, heavier than anyone else's on the crew given his size, sounded on the stairs. "That's where I put it last night."

"Are you sure?"

"I did the say-it-three-times-out-loud trick."

"He did. I heard him." Kayla must have been set up in the living room. "And I saw him put the key there. I haven't touched it."

"Lex, Trev?" Ryan's shout was clearly aimed up the stairs. "Either of you have the van key?"

Two voices called, "No" from upstairs a moment before a door opened and shut. "Man, what smells so good?" Lexi asked.

Hannah exchanged a grin with Lacy. "Cinnamon rolls," she called, aiming her head in the direction of the kitchen door.

A stampede commenced. Or at least that was what it sounded like as five pairs of feet pounded over hardwood floors. Kayla, no doubt the closest if she'd been in the living room, got there first, followed quickly by Ryan and Oran, and then the Stokleys.

Hannah laughed. "Lacy's still icing them. You can grab coffee now if you want, but we'll need a few more minutes before anything else is ready." She poured the steaming coffee into the carafes that would seal in the heat.

Most of the group moved to the coffee station, but Oran lingered near the exit to the hallway, hands on hips. "Key, guys. If we can't find it, no filming today."

Kayla had always been no-nonsense about her coffee. She already held a full cup as she strode toward Oran. "I'll grab the spare from my bag while we look for it."

Oran stared at her. "There's a spare?"

"How long have I known you guys, and how many things have you lost over the course of the show?" Kayla asked with a laugh. "Of course I've got a spare. Give me a minute."

Oran looked at each of them. "If none of us took the key and two people saw it go into the bowl by the door, then where is it?" He frowned. "This place isn't haunted, is it?"

Lexi rolled her eyes. "Seriously, Oran. Ghosts are not the answer to everything."

"Hey, mock if you want. I was a skeptic too until Ryan put me in that ring in the forest in Transylvania. Let a spirit knock you sideways once and see how you feel then."

Lacy sent a questioning look Hannah's way, but she could only shrug. She had, in fact, been hanging out with Ryan's original crew when they'd filmed that episode of *Uncover the Unknown,* so she could attest to the fact that Oran was genuinely shaken by whatever had happened to him during that filming. He'd gone from being the one poking fun about all the bizarre stories they'd investigated to being the first to proclaim absolutely everything as haunted. Kayla, however—who had also been there—remained convinced that Oran had gotten disoriented in the fog and stumbled.

Hannah agreed with Kayla but wasn't about to get into an argument with Oran about it. In her view, God was certainly capable of the miraculous, but most things had reasonable explanations.

Like missing keys. Clearly someone had moved it, maybe without even thinking about it. "Anything else get put in that bowl?" Hannah asked as she abandoned her boxes of equipment and moved instead to the fridge. She'd brought an array of fresh fruit, yogurt, and hard-boiled eggs to supplement the pastries and needed to get them plated.

The crew turned to her, brows raised.

"Well? If someone put something else in there and then grabbed that something else out—or thought they did—they could have picked up the van key by mistake. Right?"

"See? Told you Hannah was more than a talented chef." Ryan pulled out a chair at the table and sat, coffee in hand. "I put the house key there too."

"House key is still there," Oran said. "Though why is there a key at all? I saw a keypad on the door."

"It's one of those weird ones that requires an app and can only be put on two phones. There are physical keys as backup." Ryan took a sip and gave a contented sigh. "This is good coffee. Where did you say it's from?"

"Jump Start Coffee, on Main Street." Lacy swirled the last dollop of icing over the buns with a flourish and licked the knife clean before tossing it in the sink. "Definitely a local favorite, though they close at five, so don't think you can get an after-dinner pick-me-up there. Closed on Sundays too."

Ryan turned in his chair. "Oh, hey, new face. Sorry. Cannot be expected to observe basic things before coffee." He stood, moving toward Lacy with his hand outstretched. "I'm Ryan Hall."

Hannah buried a smile in the cabinet she opened in search of a serving platter. As if Lacy didn't know who he was.

But her friend moved to intercept Ryan with a smile that didn't look nearly as fangirl as Hannah expected. "Lacy Minyard. Hannah's oldest friend, owner of Bluegrass Hollow Farm, stand-in sous-chef for the week, and fan of the show. Not as big a fan as my history-nerd husband, but still a fan."

"Hannah always talked about you nonstop," Ryan said, smiling and shaking Lacy's hand emphatically.

Lacy shot Hannah an exaggerated glare. "Hannah *completely* neglected to mention that she knew famous people, and I've yet to forgive her for it."

Hannah set the largest plate she could find on the counter and reached for the bags and cartons of fruit. "I hadn't talked to Ryan in years. And Kayla isn't technically famous."

"Nor does Kayla ever intend to be." Kayla strode back in, spare van key in hand. She passed it off to Oran and then made a beeline for Lacy. "Hi. I'm Kayla Dreher, the one who actually bothered to keep in touch with our girl, and I've wanted to meet you for ages."

"Hannah has mentioned you plenty. I feel like I already know you." Lacy ducked past Kayla's outstretched hand for a hug.

Kayla laughed and hugged her back. "I feel the same way."

Ryan pretended to pout. "I see how it is. Little ol' Ryan doesn't rate."

Everyone cracked up at the thought of the bear-size Ryan being *little* anything.

Hannah found her mind wandering back to the years she'd lived in California and the calls and emails she and Lacy had exchanged. "You know, I bet I did mention him and Oran at some point, Lacy. I told you about the time I got stranded in San Francisco on a weekend trip, right? When the car broke down?" As she spoke, she snipped bunches of grapes and arranged them on the plate.

Lacy retrieved plates from a cupboard. "Yeah, I think so. That was when you were almost mugged, right?"

A story that was funny in retrospect had been anything but at the time. "That's the one. And I was with Kayla, Ryan, Oran, and Cath, who has since moved on to other things. Ryan was the one who scared the guy off. So I'm sure I mentioned them by name." She shot a grin at Ryan. "Only, Ryan wasn't *Ryan Hall* yet."

Kayla snorted and moved to the table. "He was always Ryan Hall. It's just that people didn't pay to see him be an utter goofball back then. Did he tell you he's doing a live comedy tour next year?"

"No, but I can picture it." After an hour with Ryan, he'd have everyone rolling. She reached for the strawberries and added them to the plate. She'd already prewashed the fruit that morning.

The front door opened and shut again, and a moment later Oran came into the kitchen, a perplexed expression on his face. He held up two identical key fobs. "Well, I found the missing key. It was locked in the van."

Kayla regarded him with pursed lips.

Ryan shook his head. "I put it in the bowl."

"He did," Kayla said again. "I saw him do it. Someone must have gone out to the van last night." She glanced over at Lexi and Trevor.

They both shook their heads. "We went from the living room straight upstairs," Lexi insisted. "Haven't been in the van since we got back from dinner."

Oran scrunched up his nose. "Anyone sleepwalk? If not, I'm gonna go with the ghost theory."

Kayla snorted, but she looked more amused than annoyed. "Not a ghost. Clearly, we're just misremembering the order of things."

"All of us?" Oran dropped both keys on the counter and headed for the coffee station. Rather than coffee, he selected one of the herbal tea bags Hannah had set out and poured hot water from one of the carafes.

Kayla shrugged, leaned against the counter, and plucked a strawberry from the plate with a grin. "Whatever. You found the key, and all is well. Is it still raining?"

"A little, and the air is cool." Oran reached for the bottle of honey and squeezed some into his tea. "Wouldn't hurt my feelings if we waited a while before we get started out there."

"Dealing with rain gear for all the cameras is a pain," Kayla said to Hannah and Lacy. "Though we do it when we have to. The weather does not always play nice with our schedule."

Made sense. Hannah added orange and kiwi slices to the platter, followed by pineapple chunks, and then handed the plate to Kayla. "If you would? For breakfast we'll take everything to the table. I'll set up lunch buffet style."

"The woman has cinnamon rolls and thinks we'll eat fruit. Adorable." But Kayla took the plate with a wink.

Hannah pointed at her. "You were just eating strawberries."

"Because the cinnamon rolls weren't in front of me yet."

"The cinnamon rolls won't fill you up for long if you're tromping around outside." Hannah pulled the bowl of peeled eggs from the fridge, along with a selection of Greek yogurts in multiple flavors. "Add some protein," she advised as she slid them onto the table too.

Ryan arched a brow at her. "Seriously? You recommend protein and offer eggs and yogurt? It's like you don't even know me."

With a grin, she spun back to the insulated bag she'd left on the counter, unzipped it, and brought out the dish of bacon and sausage links she'd cooked at home. "Still warm," she said as she put them on the table too.

"Ah, there it is. We *are* still friends." Ryan pointed to the two empty place settings. "I hope that means you two are joining us."

"Unless we'd be in the way, if you're going over call sheets or something." Hannah met Kayla's gaze and smiled. "Look at me, using the lingo."

"I'm so proud." Kayla gestured toward the empty seats. "Sit. Eat. I'll wait until everybody's gotten the icing wiped off their fingers before I pass out the paperwork anyway. And it's not like anything is confidential."

"In fact, we love picking the brains of locals." Ryan leaned out of the way so Lacy could slide the two hot pans of rolls onto the trivets already awaiting them on the table. "Have either of you ever heard about this missing diamond?"

Hannah shook her head along with Lacy. "Not until Kayla mentioned it. Which is weird, right? How big did you say it was?"

"Close to thirty carats." Kayla accepted the spatula Lacy handed her, lifted the first roll from the pan, and slid it onto Ryan's plate.

Hannah poured herself some coffee and moved to take the seat beside Lacy. She paused before she sat. "Oh, we have juice too. Apple, orange, and grapefruit. Anyone want any?"

Everyone declined in one way or another, so Hannah sat. Kayla finished serving the rolls.

"So a thirty-carat diamond is seriously thought to be hidden around here, and we locals don't know about it?" Hannah mused. "That seems a bit odd."

"Agreed. What's the story there?" Lacy took two slices of bacon from the dish and then handed it to Hannah.

"Well, I was searching for mysteries in Barren County, and I saw an article from 1910 that caught my eye." Kayla, despite her teasing, put a good assortment of fruit on her plate. "Apparently an outlaw named Franklin Sullivan stole this diamond from an associate in Arkansas and then somehow made it to Kentucky on foot."

Lacy leaned in, eyes alight. "To this county?"

"To this house—or that's my bet, anyway." Kayla grinned. "I tried to find out why this guy would travel so far, and I discovered that his sister had married a Kentucky man and moved here with him."

Ryan tapped a finger on the table. "As in, moved *here*. The sister's married name was Elinor Payne."

Hannah had already gleaned that much from the questions Ryan had asked Ford yesterday, but Lacy's eyes went wide. "So this outlaw thought he'd hide out with his sister?"

"That's our best guess." Kayla shrugged. "His reasons were never reported, but then, his relationship with Elinor Payne was never reported either. The only thing the newspaper article said was that the law caught up to him somewhere in the countryside surrounding Blackberry Valley, and he was shot and killed. The diamond was never recovered."

"So while it's feasible that he stashed it somewhere along the way from Kimberly, Arkansas, to Blackberry Valley, Kentucky, that seems unlikely." Ryan put an egg on his plate beside his meat. "Given the timeline, he would have been booking it. He made really good time for being on foot, which doesn't lend itself to theories of him taking the time to hide something well and mark it so he could find it later."

"It's far more likely that he stashed it around here somewhere." Kayla glanced around, presumably to see if everyone was done filling their plates, then held out her hands to say grace. She smiled. "And, God willing, we'll figure out where."

Chapter Seven

S o what do you think?" Lacy asked as they meandered down Main
Street two hours later, aimed for Neil's bookstore, Legend & Key.
"You think this diamond is really hidden somewhere nearby?"

Hannah shrugged. The rain had stopped, and the sun tried to
push through the clouds, but she was glad she'd worn a lightweight
jacket. "I have no idea. But it could be, right? I do agree with Ryan
that it makes more sense than his leaving it somewhere along the
way. He obviously thought he'd find a safe harbor with his sister."

"Yeah." Lacy didn't sound convinced. "But that article Kayla
showed us after breakfast was vague at best. It didn't say where he
was when the law caught up with him, didn't mention he had family
here. Are we sure it's the same Franklin Sullivan who was Elinor's
brother?"

"What are the chances of a different Franklin Sullivan showing
up in Elinor's neighborhood?" Hannah bumped their shoulders
together. "I think they're right about him seeking her out, probably
hoping for a place to hide."

She and Lacy had listened to the debrief around the table after
breakfast while they put the perishables away and Hannah finished
unpacking her supplies. They had chimed in now and then when
the crew had questions about the area, but otherwise they merely
listened. When the production team went off to get the lay of the

land, Hannah and Lacy offered to ask some likely sources in town if they had any information, since Hannah wanted to be at the restaurant at ten anyway to sign for a delivery she needed for the crew's lunch. They weren't eating until one, though, so she still had plenty of time.

Legend & Key made sense as a first stop—not just because Lacy's husband was as likely as anyone else to know the local lore, but also because the crew hoped to find some old maps of the area and Neil definitely had those. Hannah and Lacy had volunteered to run that errand, stop in at the library, and get in touch with the head of the historical society too.

Lacy led the way into the store, the bell over the door announcing their presence.

Neil looked up from his place behind the counter, a grin quickly emerging when he spotted his wife. "Hey. Thought you two were busy with the famous people this morning. What brings you to my neck of the woods?"

"We're here on official *Destination Discovery* business," Lacy announced with a grin. "They need maps."

"Ah. Couldn't find what they need online?" Neil walked toward the section of the store that housed his passion collection.

"Apparently not." Hannah followed the Minyards, shrugging out of her jacket as she went. "Do you have anything from the 1910 range? Town and surrounding areas?"

"Maybe even the whole county." Lacy leaned against the wall as Neil pulled a drawer open. "We're not sure where Sullivan was caught. We're assuming it was near the old Payne place, but obviously we don't know for sure."

A thump and a muted squeal from one of the aisles made Neil turn, brows raised. "Are you okay, Mrs. Bryant?"

"I'm fine. Sorry, Neil. Book just jumped right out of my hands." A sixtysomething woman stepped into view, cheeks flushed in clear embarrassment. Her silver bob looked a bit messy with one side trying to work free of its clip, and her shirt was only half tucked in. She waved a book in one hand. "Found what I was looking for though." She edged a bit closer, her expression shifting. "Did you say Sullivan? And Payne?"

Hannah tried to place the woman's face and name. And, for that matter, the dishevelment. Those were familiar, but it wasn't until she imagined the woman with darker hair and a slimmer figure that she realized why. "Mrs. Bryant, as in our middle school science teacher?"

Mrs. Bryant peered through her glasses at Hannah for a long moment, then beamed. "Hannah Prentiss! I'd heard you were back in the area, but I don't make it back to Blackberry Valley as often as I used to. I retired to Cave City, you see. And like I keep trying to tell Neil, you can call me Rhiannon now. I'm not your teacher anymore."

But Hannah couldn't bring herself to do any such thing. It felt disrespectful. "I didn't know you'd retired, but I hope you're enjoying it."

"Most days, yes. Though I do miss the kids." Mrs. Bryant tilted her head. "I hear you opened a restaurant. Right?"

"That's right. The Hot Spot. It's in the building that used to be the firehouse."

Neil looked to be holding back a smile. "Are you ready to check out, Mrs. Bryant? If so, Lacy can help you while I search for maps."

"I am, yes. Thank you, Lacy, dear." Mrs. Bryant fell in behind Lacy on the way to the checkout counter. But the teacher glanced over her shoulder at Hannah. "Y'all are asking about the old Sullivan and Payne story? And did I hear you mention *Destination Discovery*?"

Hannah's brows rose. "You know the show?"

"Of course I do. Did you see their special on the pyramids a few years ago?" Mrs. Bryant reached up to tuck her hair behind her ear, which only made it slip more from its clip. "To get to see a tomb opened like that for the first time must be an archaeologist's dream."

Hannah had seen that episode before she moved home. "Very cool. I'm doing the food for the production team, and Lacy's lending me a hand. I'm friends with the show's head researcher. We went to the same church in LA when I lived there." Now, the important thing. "You know the story about Franklin Sullivan?"

Mrs. Bryant slid a bestselling thriller onto the counter and pursed her lips. "It does sound familiar."

Hannah wasn't buying the nonchalant tone. The woman had dropped her book and repeated the names as if they meant something to her.

Lacy scanned the book and read off the price.

Mrs. Bryant tapped her credit card against the reader, and it beeped its approval.

Hannah wished her friend had taken a bit more time. "If you're familiar with the story about the outlaw and the diamond he's rumored to have left in the area, Ryan Hall would love to chat with you. He's searching for locals to help direct him to likely hiding places." If Mrs. Bryant was a fan of the show, maybe that would keep her here for a few more minutes.

A spark lit in her eyes. "Well, now. I'll have to see what I can dig up. My grandfather told a few tales, though we'll have to see if I can find any record of them." Taking the bag Lacy had just slid the book into, Mrs. Bryant started toward the door. "Thanks, Neil," she called. "See you next time."

"That was odd," Hannah muttered to Lacy.

Lacy chuckled. "You do remember Mrs. Bryant, don't you? How we always tried to get out of the lesson by distracting her with some tangent or other? She's always been the epitome of the absent-minded professor."

"But she also has a memory like a steel trap," Neil put in from where he stood with the drawers of maps. "It might take her a while to sort through all the random factoids she's learned over the years, but I bet she'll come back with something soon. The geology and earth science units were always her favorites, if you recall. Ah, here we go." Neil lifted a folded paper. "This should be the one you need."

A few minutes later, Hannah and Lacy left the shop again, receipt in hand to give to Kayla for reimbursement. They'd have to drive to the library, so they aimed for the Subaru Hannah had parked behind the restaurant. They were still a minute's walk away when her phone rang. She paused to dig it out of her purse and smiled at her father's name on the screen. She swiped to accept the call and raised the phone to her ear. "Hi, Dad."

"Hey, sweetie. What's this I hear about you hobnobbing with movie stars?"

Hannah laughed. She'd sent Dad a text the day before but hadn't had time for a phone call. "TV star, not movie stars. You remember me talking about Kayla and Ryan and Oran, don't you? When I lived in California?"

"Sure do. I tried watching that first show of theirs and just couldn't get into it. I like the new one though. Don't suppose the crew wants to come over for dinner sometime, do they? I'd love to meet them. I don't think they were in town that time I visited you out there." That seemed to be the case every time someone had come to see her. "Gordon and I can fire up the grill. You know I make a mean burger." Uncle Gordon was her father's brother. They lived together in Hannah's childhood home with Dad's border terrier, Zeus.

"You certainly do. And I can ask them. Do you have a day in mind?"

"Well, I ran to the store this morning and got enough hamburger to feed a small army, and I happen to know Drew and Allison and the kids are free tonight. No worries, though, because I can I always freeze the patties with no harm done."

She already had chicken marinating for dinner, but it would be fine to use tomorrow. In fact, it would probably taste even better. But she couldn't speak for the whole crew. "I'll run the offer by them and let you know as soon as I can, okay?"

"Sure, no pressure. You with them now?"

"No, I'm running some errands with Lacy."

"She and Neil are welcome to come to dinner too. And Liam, of course. You're still making time for him, aren't you?"

A smile tugged at her lips again. To say Dad was a big fan of Liam was an understatement. "He came over to my place last night to help me prep fruit and veggies for today and is planning on helping me with the dinner shift each evening he's free. Not exactly dates, but still time together."

"Good. I know you two sometimes have trouble getting your schedules to line up. You know, if you just got married—"

"Dad." The name emerged on a groan. Yes, she'd begun dreaming of a happily-ever-after with Liam, especially since they'd exchanged I-love-you's. And yes, she found herself hoping it would happen sooner rather than later.

But she wasn't about to push Liam. She'd watched enough other relationships implode to know pressure wasn't the best thing for them.

Dad chuckled. "I know, I know. I just want my girl to be happy."

"I am happy."

"But you could be even happier. Anyway, let me know about dinner. I'll bake some cookies, just in case."

Lacy must have been able to hear Dad from where she walked at Hannah's side, because she was obviously trying to keep from laughing.

Hannah shook her head. "Well, that's probably incentive enough to get the sound engineer to vote yes. Cookies are her favorite."

"Great. We'll do some hand-cut fries too. Gordon's gotten good at using that little deep fryer. You think six o'clock will work?"

Lacy's laugh escaped, and Hannah's did too. "Cart before the horse, Dad. I'll let you know, okay?"

"Sure. Talk to you soon, honey."

They disconnected, and Hannah shook her head. "Guess I need to talk to Kayla now."

Lacy, still chuckling, held out her hand. "I'll drive, and you can play party planner."

Hannah climbed into the passenger side of her Subaru before dialing Kayla's number. A call seemed more expedient than a text, if they were really going to be making plans.

"Hey, Hannah," Kayla said on the second ring. "What's up? Find the map okay? Have questions?"

"We have what you need. I'm calling because my dad is eager to meet you guys and wanted to invite the crew over for dinner sometime."

"Sweet. We're in. We love meeting locals, and your family's lived here forever, right?"

"Pretty much."

"Great. We'd love to meet your dad anyway, but the potential for prying local history from him makes it even better. Name the day."

And here came the trickier part. "It sounds like he'd really like it to be tonight. I know that's short notice, of course—"

"Actually, that's perfect. We're not doing any filmed investigation yet, which makes it easier to stop at a given time. Assuming that doesn't mess with whatever you've got planned for dinner?"

"My plans will keep until tomorrow. No problem."

"Then we're a yes."

Hannah's shoulders relaxed. "Awesome. You don't need to run it by the others or anything?"

"No, they're used to me dictating their every move."

From somewhere in the background, Hannah heard Ryan call out, "Everyone knows she's the real boss of this operation. No one even dares breathe without her say-so."

"Be glad I'm a benevolent tyrant," Kayla said to him. "Now get back to work."

Hannah laughed. It was fun being around them again. "Six o'clock okay for dinner? Or later, given the late-ish lunch?"

"Six should be fine. We'll be tromping through the fields around here this afternoon in search of good camera shots, so we'll be hungry again."

"Great. I'll let Dad know. He's making his amazing burgers, my uncle's doing homemade fries, and I hear there are cookies planned. In case anyone asks."

"Oh, they will. And that menu will please everybody. Tell your dad I can't wait to meet him. And thanks for picking up the map."

"We'll be back with it soon."

Hannah was about to say goodbye, but Ryan's voice in the background got louder. "Okay, this is getting ridiculous. Have you seen the Jeep key?"

"You put it in the bowl last night," Kayla replied. "With the van key."

"Yeah, I know. But it's not there now. Don't suppose you've got a spare one of that too, do you?"

Hannah frowned. *Two* keys missing from the same place at the same time? That was more than a coincidence.

Then a thought popped into her mind. "Check the Jeep."

"What?" Kayla asked.

"The van keys were in the van. See if the Jeep keys are in the Jeep."

Footsteps sounded on the other side, and Ryan asked, "Where are you going?"

"Obeying Hannah's hunch," Kayla said. A door creaked, and the sound of the steps changed. A moment later, a disbelieving laugh came over the line. "Yep. There they are in the center console." A car door opened. "Perfect. I thought this one was too new to let the key be locked inside. The van has an actual ignition key, but this has the proximity thing."

Ryan's voice came again. "Okay, the van key being in the van I could let go, assuming someone forgot they ran back out. But for both keys to be missing, and in different vehicles? No. This isn't a coincidence, and it wasn't forgetfulness either."

"So, what? A prank?" Kayla sounded dubious. "Phil's the resident prankster, and he's not here. Another camera operator," she added, more directly into the phone for Hannah's benefit. "And he's absolutely the kind that would pull this sort of joke just to laugh at us scratching our heads."

"Maybe he flew in separately and is sneaking around. Phil?" Ryan's steps moved off.

Kayla laughed. "It's not Phil. His daughter's birthday is this week, remember? That's why he bowed out of coming."

"Or maybe he just said it was so he could trick us."

Hannah laughed along with Kayla. "All right, we're pulling into the library. I'll talk to you when we get back."

"Sure. And thanks."

Hannah said goodbye and hung up, quickly explaining what was going on to Lacy when her friend shot her a questioning look.

Lacy handed Hannah her keys and climbed out of the car. "That's plain weird. I mean, unless this Phil character really did sneak in behind them to play a prank. Which is also weird, but also hilarious. That would be true dedication to a bit."

"More believable than a ghost anyway. At any rate, I'd better let Dad know that dinner tonight is a go. You and Neil are invited too, if you feel like burgers and fries and cookies." She pulled up her text thread with her dad to send a quick affirmative.

"That's not even hard. I know Neil will love meeting the crew. I'll let him know."

They both paused outside the library's front doors. Hannah sent a message to Liam too, to let him know the change of plans, and he quickly confirmed as well.

"Neil will meet me at your dad's." Lacy slid her phone into her pocket and reached for the door. "Let's go find some more local contacts."

Hannah moved to follow but paused with a sigh when her phone rang again. Odd—it was Kayla again. "Hey."

"Hey, I just got a call from Ford's daughter, Brooke. You know, the one he warned us not to feel we needed to indulge. Do you know her by chance? Is she reliable?"

Brooke Payne. Hannah thought about it for a minute but came up blank. "Doesn't sound familiar, though given Ford's age, she's probably a good bit younger than me. Why?"

"Well, she says she knows where Franklin Sullivan was hiding out—and that she can take us there tomorrow."

Chapter Eight

Elinor set the percolator on the stove. Catching movement in the predawn gray out the window, she went to the door to quietly open it. She'd lain awake more than she'd slept, but even so, she probably felt better this morning than her brother would after sleeping in her cellar.

He slipped silently onto the porch, blankets and pillow folded neatly in his arms. When she held the door open for him, he came inside, his gaze moving toward the ceiling. "Judah still asleep?" he whispered.

She pulled the door closed again to keep the brisk spring air outside. "Yes. He'll probably sleep another hour or two. Have a seat, and I'll get you breakfast."

Franklin shook his head. "I want to be gone before full daylight. Just point me in a likely direction for a place to lie low for a few days and get some rest, and I'll be out of your hair."

Narrowing her eyes, she pointed at the chair he'd occupied last night. "Sit."

Her brother's shoulders sagged, but he also smiled. "Fine. But only for a minute. I'm serious about not bringing any danger your way."

She waved that off. "If anyone's coming, I'll see them long before they get here." She nodded to the window that gave her a fine view of the long driveway. "You can always slip out the back and get to the tree line, with the house blocking their view the whole time. But you need food. What have you been eating?"

He shrugged. "What I could hunt or scavenge, mostly. Not the best time of year for that, I grant you."

And Franklin was a city boy, not a man who'd grown up hunting or fishing. There wasn't a lot of call for either in Chicago. Which explained how tired he looked and the way his clothes hung on him. How long had he been on the run?

"Well, I've been up for an hour already, baking," she said softly. "And I fetched some ham and a rope of sausage links for you from the smokehouse. You'll have to eat the baked goods within a few days, but the smoked meat should last. And I think we have some hardtack in the pantry. Tom would take it on hunting trips, since it keeps forever and is easy to pack. You'll have to soak it in water to avoid chipping a tooth, of course."

Franklin's gaze drifted to the pack she motioned toward. Would he guess that it had been Tom's, that she'd thought long and hard about parting with it before she began stuffing it with food?

Silly, that. She had to believe that whatever mess Franklin was in right now, he'd work it out. She'd see him again at their parents' house in Chicago in a year or two, or he'd come here to Kentucky to visit under more normal circumstances. He'd give her back the pack and explain what in the world had happened.

And if he didn't, it was just a bag. She had more important things to remember her husband by. Like Judah.

"You didn't have to go to all that trouble, Ellie," Franklin murmured. "Not when I haven't even answered your questions."

"I don't need you to," she said, trying to convince herself as well as him. "You're my brother. If I came to you needing help, you wouldn't ask why."

He smiled, and for a second he looked like he was supposed to—steady, loving, unwavering, and always filled with joy. "Oh, I'd ask plenty of questions. I'd just help you regardless of the answers."

She moved to his side and rested a hand on his shoulder. "And so will I." Then she added a grin of her own. "Though if you wanted to provide some of those answers, I wouldn't complain."

His smile faded. "Maybe when it's safe for you to know. I need to make sure no one's followed me here first. I think I've lost them, but I can't be sure."

It was on the tip of her tongue to ask which *them* he was referring to, but she bit it back. He wouldn't answer.

So then. "I've been thinking about where you can go."

He perked up. "Yeah? I thought Tom mentioned a hunting lodge at one point. Is that nearby?"

She grimaced. "About two hours west, but I wouldn't go there if I were you. Tom's cousins use it frequently. For all I know, someone's there now. Seems like one relative or another is always going there for a week, and they often do this time of year."

Franklin sagged again. "Yeah, that doesn't sound ideal."

"I don't know of a place to send you that would have any degree of luxury, but..."

"But?" He met her gaze, hope sparking anew in his.

And that was Franklin too, always ready to hope. How could he still be that person, full of hope and optimism and ready to protect *her*, if he was all the things that newspaper article had accused him of being?

She drew in a long breath. "There are a lot of caves in the area. Including one not far from here that would serve your needs well, I think. There's a spring inside, so you'd have fresh water. And it's hard to find if you don't know it's there, so it's unlikely anyone would stumble across you by accident."

Franklin thought for a moment, then said, "That would do nicely. Think I can find it on my own?"

"It's possible." She hadn't visited it herself in years, not since before Judah was born. But she thought she could find it again. "If you head due north for a quarter of a mile, following the stream that goes by our property right behind the tree line, you'll see a place where a giant tree fell across the stream. It's huge, easily five feet in diameter. Use that to cross to the other side and then look for a double-trunk tree growing around a rock. The entrance to the cave is right behind it. From a distance it appears to be nothing more than a split in the rock of the hillside, but it's bigger than it seems when you get up to it. You'll fit through the opening, and it widens up a lot about ten feet in."

He nodded along with her instructions. "That sounds perfect. And other locals don't know about it?"

She shrugged. "I can't say that definitively, but Tom said he'd never seen anyone else around there. We never found anything inside it to hint at other people visiting it."

"Animal life?"

"No evidence of it when I was last there, though it's been a while. Tom said he used it as a hideout when he was a boy, though, and he never ran into anything."

"Good to know. I'm not really feeling up to fighting off bears or mountain lions." Even his smile seemed tired.

The coffee started boiling, brown liquid bubbling up into the clear knob of the percolator's lid. She liked hers a little stronger than her brother did, so she went ahead and poured him a cup, then put it back on the heat for another couple of minutes. "Here." She set the mug in front of him and nudged the sugar bowl forward. "Mother always says the world is better after a good cup of coffee."

He took a sip, eyes sliding closed. "She's a wise woman, that mother of ours."

"I can send some coffee with you too, and my old percolator. It has a few dents, but it works fine. Tom's sister gave me a new one for Christmas last year."

He frowned. "Think a fire is wise?"

"I'm not sure where the cave's vents are, to be honest. We built a fire in it once when we were out exploring and got caught in the rain, but we couldn't see the smoke from the cave anywhere nearby. Tom checked out of curiosity before we put it out. He was hoping to find a bigger way in, but he never did." As she spoke, she fetched the old percolator from the pantry, along with some coffee.

"Sounds like that's in my favor." He took another sip, then stood. "I'd better get moving. The sun will be up soon."

"Take the blankets and pillow. It'll be cool in the cave. We won't miss them here."

He paused and met her gaze. "You sure?"

"Of course I'm sure." She just wished she could do more. "Anything you need me to do? People to watch for, maybe?"

"Absolutely not," he replied sharply. "You need to pretend you haven't seen me."

"All right, calm down. I won't seek anything out." But she'd listen to whatever people in town were saying. "Judah will be spending the day with his cousin tomorrow. I'll come to the cave with some more food."

"Ellie—"

"Don't argue. I go for solitary picnics all the time. Anyone who sees me won't think anything of it." And if he really thought she was going to send him off into the woods and not check on him, he didn't know her half as well as he thought he did.

His sigh of resignation reassured her. "All right. Thanks." He leaned down to press a kiss to her cheek, finished his coffee, and moved to retrieve the pack in the corner. He hefted it onto his shoulder, then gathered the pillow and blankets again. "I owe you, Ellie."

"You do not. We're family." Mustering a smile, she held the door open for him and tried to imbue her expression with encouragement. She thought she managed it until he was off the porch and striding toward the tree line. Once certain he wasn't going to look back, she let the cheer fall and quietly closed the door again.

She wasn't like those pitiable creatures she read about in the newspaper, was she? The ones who aided and abetted criminals because they couldn't believe that a loved one would ever be party to something so abhorrent? Or, worse, the ones who paid the price for their naivete when those relatives robbed them blind or murdered them?

"Don't be ridiculous." She turned back to her cozy kitchen. Franklin was no criminal. And even if he was, he'd never hurt her or Judah.

She picked up his mug, walked to the stove, and topped it off with the stronger coffee. After setting the percolator onto the warming spot at the rear of the stove so it didn't boil anymore, she added a dollop of cream to the mug and took her own first sip. Then, for the first time since she'd given up on sleep over an hour ago, she went about her normal morning routine. Coffee, her Bible, and quiet.

By the time Judah came flying down the stairs with his usual boundless energy, she could almost convince herself the two encounters with her brother had been her imagination. He couldn't really be on the run from the law. Couldn't have spent the night in her cellar. Couldn't even now be hiding in the cave she hadn't thought about in years. Could he?

Judah, as usual, climbed into her lap the moment he entered the kitchen. "Guess what I dreamed, Mama?"

Her chest went tight. If he'd dreamed of his uncle, having heard their whispers, she wasn't sure what she'd do. How could she protect him from the situation with Franklin without lying to him? "What, baby?"

"I dreamed the big rock in the field was a head. And it started talking to me and told me a story about those dinosaur bones you were telling me about the other day. You know, the ones you and Daddy saw in the music thing?"

How could she ever contain a smile around this boy? "The museum?"

"Yeah, that. And then the bones showed up. And the dinosaur did a dance like Rudy was doing the other day and..."

She let him continue the tale as she got up to fix his breakfast, asking questions here and there and laughing at his antics. And, yes, wishing her brother could be here truly. Here at the table, egging on Judah's chatter and chiming in with his own stories. Judah adored Franklin, despite how rare their visits were. But her brother always sent the best gifts—in Judah's eyes anyway. Half his rock collection had come courtesy of Franklin. New geodes or fossils were always showing up addressed to her little boy.

Her hands paused on the loaf of bread she was cutting. She'd always wondered how Franklin could afford to send such gifts so regularly but had chalked it up to his frugal living and lack of wife and children of his own. But was it something darker? Such as bribes or illicit funds from the Irish Mafia?

No. No, that couldn't be it.

She finished cutting the bread, set it in the oven to toast while she fried an egg just the way Judah liked it, and made one for herself as well. They ate, went about their chores, had their daily reading lesson—a normal day, if she could ignore the cloud hovering at the back of her mind.

Wondering if Franklin had found the cave. Wondering if he was warm enough. Wondering if he'd sneak into the house after dark.

Wondering if whoever was after him would show up here.

She had her answer as the sun neared the western horizon, spilling red-gold light onto the driveway. She stood in the kitchen again, peeling potatoes for their dinner, when movement once again caught her attention out the window.

Not her brother sneaking out of the cellar this time. No, this was a man on horseback coming up the drive. She watched for a minute, telling herself he must be a neighbor.

But none of the neighbors had a white horse like that, nor sat so tall in the saddle. She set down a potato, half-peeled. Where was Judah? Outside? He came and went as he willed in the afternoons, and she never stopped him from exploring.

He knew to stay within earshot though. She was about to call out the back door for him when she heard the familiar thump over her head of one of his rock boxes hitting the floor of his bedroom. He kept them on his bedside table but was always hefting one down to the floor to examine his collection.

She blew out a long breath. He was upstairs, safe and sound. Not that she usually minded the thought of him coming into contact with a stranger on their own property, but with Franklin's warnings about danger in her mind, that had all changed.

She washed and dried her hands, then checked the driveway again. The man and horse were closer, enough so that she was sure she didn't know him. He wore a broad hat, a long coat, and—was that glint of sunlight on metal a badge of some kind? A star, maybe?

He wasn't a local lawman. She knew the sheriff and all his deputies.

Because she'd have done it regardless, she walked through the house toward the front door and opened it, stepping out onto the porch as he drew near. The only thing that took a bit of effort was fastening a smile on her lips. "Evening," she called out, as she would to any stranger approaching her door.

"Ma'am." He drew his horse to a halt and swung out of the saddle with the ease of someone who spent more hours in it than out of it.

Gracious, but he was a tall drink of water. Even standing two steps up as she was, she had to tilt her head back to look him in the eye when he approached.

And the eyes surprised her. Not their color—a rather common shade of blue—but their kindness. She'd met plenty of lawmen over the years through her brother, and Franklin himself was the only one she'd ever found with that same gentleness shining from his eyes. Usually they were stern, intimidating, or at the very least weary.

This fellow looked road-weary but not soul-weary.

It made her want to see Franklin again, to classify his type of weariness. She hadn't thought to do so before.

Later. For now, she smiled. "Can I help you? If you're traveling through and hoping for a meal, I'll have one ready in less than an hour, and you're welcome to join us." It was her habit to make such offers.

"That's kind of you, ma'am, but I won't trouble you. I wanted to have a quick word. My name's Nathan Davis. I'm with the US Marshals."

She nodded, not knowing how else to respond. She'd never met a marshal before, but she knew they could pursue outlaws across state lines, which meant his appearance here was likely no coincidence. "Mrs. Elinor Payne."

He nodded too, but no recognition lit his eyes. Maybe that meant he didn't know her name. Or maybe it meant he knew exactly who she was and was careful to hide his reaction. "Sorry to interrupt your evening, Mrs. Payne. I'll try not to take up too much of your time. I've just come through town, asking if anyone has seen a man I'm searching for. No one has, but they suggested I ask the folks who own farms around here, since this fellow is smart enough to avoid centers of population and seek a meal or shelter from someone more isolated."

Tilting her head to the side, she searched his words for what she *should* be asking. "What sort of man?"

"About five ten," he said, indicating the height against himself. "Red-brown hair, green eyes. On the slender side. His name's Franklin Sullivan, but if he came by, I doubt he'd give you his real name."

Interesting. Unless he was testing her—which was a possibility—he didn't know she was Franklin's sister. She lifted her brows. "Is this fellow an outlaw, Marshal? Is he dangerous?"

He winced. "Well, the folks down in Arkansas seem to think so. He's wanted for murder."

"What?" Of their own volition, her hands flew upward, clutching at the shawl draped over her shoulders.

"I don't mean to alarm you, ma'am," Mr. Davis said quickly, holding up his hands in a calming gesture. "No reason at all to think he'd harm you. He's lying low, not stirring up trouble. The fellow in Arkansas was an associate of his, I'm told. Deal gone sour or some such."

She was going to have a few very pointed questions for Franklin tomorrow. For now, she forced herself to relax a bit, to swallow. "Well, I don't—"

"What color hair did the man have who was here this morning, Mama?"

She spun, wishing she'd closed the front door behind her. Judah stood at the base of the stairs, curiosity on his face rather than alarm. And then his words sank in. "What man, sweetheart?" He couldn't mean Franklin. He'd still been asleep. It had been an hour after Franklin left that Judah came downstairs.

But her little boy, with his red-brown hair—like hers, like his uncle's—came right outside and slipped his hand into hers, looking earnestly up at her with green eyes identical to Franklin's. "The man walking through the field this morning. It was still all gray out, so I couldn't see colors. He talked to you, didn't he? I thought I heard voices." Judah turned toward the marshal, a smile of such bright innocence on his face that it hurt. "My mama's always nice to folks who need help. Never turns anyone away, just like the preacher says we should do."

Guilt twisted. It was true, yes, but not so innocent in this case. She looked back to the marshal, expecting his eyes to have narrowed on her in suspicion.

Instead, he smiled at Judah and crouched down to be more on his level. "And you must be the master of the house. What's your name?"

Judah puffed up. "I'm Mr. Payne."

Mr. Davis laughed and held out a hand. "Nice to meet you, Mr. Payne. Do you remember what time this fellow walked through your field?"

Judah shook the marshal's hand, then looked back up to her. "I don't know. I was still playing with my rocks. What time was it, Mama?"

The marshal's gaze focused on her again too, and he straightened.

She made a show of thinking. "Oh, that must have been...I don't know exactly. Six thirty or seven? Not quite daylight yet, like you said. But this man had dark hair." Not a lie. As dirty as Franklin's hair had been, it was nothing like his natural auburn.

Still, interest sparked in Mr. Davis's eyes. "You spoke to him? Did he have an accent? This fellow's from Chicago."

She fully expected Judah to proclaim that his mama's family was from Chicago, but instead he said, "Say, that's a pretty horse. Can I pet him?"

Bless him.

The marshal gave her boy another smile. "You sure can. Her name's Stardust, and she's as friendly as can be. Approach her from the left and give her nose a good rub, and she'll be your friend forever."

Judah grinned and trotted away.

Mr. Davis's gaze returned to her. "Did you notice an accent, Mrs. Payne?"

Again, she could answer honestly. "I didn't." She wouldn't, of course, having heard the clipped Chicago tones most of her life, even if her family had teased her endlessly about picking up the Southern drawl so quickly after moving here. She'd joked that it was contagious, so they'd better watch out or they too would be talking like Tom by the end of a week's visit.

The marshal's shoulders sank a degree. "Did he give you a name?"

She shook her head. Again, technically true, though she'd have to do some soul-searching later to see if deceiving with truth would displease the Lord. But God wouldn't want her to turn an innocent man in for crimes he didn't commit, would He?

Assuming he was innocent. She believed it. Yet she had to admit there was a seed of doubt deep inside, in that place that couldn't square the brother she knew with the one she'd caught sneaking into her kitchen last night.

Mr. Davis sighed and nodded. "Thank you. Did you see which direction he was walking? Through the fields?"

It wouldn't narrow it down—there were fields all around them. She waved generally toward the back of the house, since if Judah decided to pipe in again, he'd say as much. "That way, but I didn't watch him more than a moment. I gave him some food and then returned to my morning routine." She let her brows scrunch together. "Was that wrong of me?"

The question hammered incessantly at the back of her mind.

The marshal offered her a kind smile. "It's never wrong to feed the hungry, ma'am. The Lord told us to do that, didn't He? And even to visit those in prison. So even if it was a criminal you gave food to, tending to his basic needs is never wrong. Even criminals deserve dignity as human beings."

A smile touched her lips against her will. If someone had to be hunting her brother, she could be grateful it was this man. He didn't seem like the type to shoot first and ask questions later. "Thank you for that."

He tipped his hat. "If he shows up again—I doubt he will, but if he does—would you let me know? I'll be staying at the hotel in town for a couple of days to give Stardust here a rest and get her reshoed. Or if you think of anything else, leave a note at the front desk for me."

Franklin wouldn't be coming back to the house. She'd make sure of that by finding him at the cave instead. Which this man did *not* need to know. She smiled a bit more and nodded. Glanced at Judah, who was crooning to the horse and rubbing her nose. "Thank you," she said softly, nodding toward her son so the marshal would know what she meant.

His smile was warm, sincere. "No need to thank me." He returned to Stardust and Judah, hand extended. "Nice to meet you, Mr. Payne."

Judah gave the horse one last rub and shook the marshal's hand. "Nice to meet you too, sir. Want a carrot for Stardust? We've got some." Judah's expression went sly. "She can have mine."

Laughter bubbled out of her. "Back inside with you, young man, before you give away all your vegetables." Though to the horse's owner, she added, "Though of course, I'd be happy to provide one of our *extra* carrots."

"I'll grab one!" Judah dashed inside before Mr. Davis could protest.

"Very kind of both of you. I daresay Stardust will be grateful. She does love carrots." His eyes twinkled. "Apparently more than a certain little boy."

"Doesn't take much. And again, you're welcome to join us for supper, Mr. Davis, if you have the time." Manners urged her to make the offer again, even though she knew it would complicate things to no end if he agreed.

"I do appreciate the offer, but I have several more stops to make this evening and hope to get back to town by dark." He took a step toward the horse. "I trust you'll pass the information about the outlaw on to your husband, though, so he can keep an eye out too?"

A simple enough request, and one she wouldn't have thought twice about before Tom died. Now, those offhanded, reasonable words made her shoulders draw up. "I'm a widow. But I'll pass along the warning to any neighbors I see."

He paused. Was that concern in his eyes? "A woman alone, letting a strange man inside?"

Her back went straight. "I did not let a strange man inside. I simply gave food to someone who was hungry."

His expression relaxed. Perhaps he decided to reconcile those two statements by assuming she'd left him on the porch. "I didn't mean to offend."

Judah saved her the need to respond by dashing out of the house, carrot in hand. Under Mr. Davis's supervision, he fed it to Stardust, and then the marshal mounted up, said goodbye, and turned the horse toward the road.

Elinor settled her hand on Judah's shoulder and watched him go, praying with every heartbeat that she'd done the right thing.

Chapter Nine

B ut the craziest cave I've ever been in," Ryan said that evening in Hannah's father's living room, "was the one in Ecuador. Am I right, Or?"

"It wasn't the cave," Oran protested. He sat on the floor, across from the couch that Ryan, Kayla, Trevor, and Lexi had all squeezed onto. "It was the fact that we brilliantly prepared our food in the cavern without the benefit of a tent over it, which meant that some kind of bacteria must have gotten into it. And of course Ryan and I were the only ones to get sick from it."

"How awful," Hannah said, snuggling up to Liam. They'd taken the love seat, and Dad had squeezed in on her other side with Zeus on his lap. Neil was on the floor with Oran, and Uncle Gordon was in Dad's favorite recliner. Everyone had insisted that Lacy take the remaining chair. Drew, Alison, and the kids had left twenty minutes before, thanks to school-night bedtimes.

Liam chuckled. "I saw that episode. And you know what I said when I saw the team preparing the food like that?"

"Yeah, yeah," Ryan said with a laugh. "We're all smart when we're not actually *in* the miles-long cave it takes days to hike through. We were supposed to have an awning or something set up over the food, but honestly, I don't know what happened to it. Kayla?"

"Don't look at me." Kayla was squished between Ryan and Lexi, but she didn't seem to mind. According to her, this was a frequent occurrence. "I stayed in the city for that one so I could track down an interpreter for the museum pieces of that expedition."

"That's right. And there's the problem. When Kayla's not there, everything falls apart." Ryan slung an arm around her and rubbed his knuckles into her scalp until she squealed and backed out of his embrace.

She retaliated by tickling him.

"Truce, truce!" He laughed, shoving her hands away.

Dad took a sip of his tea. "Well, let's hope whatever cave this is, it's not so big you need Hannah cooking the food inside it." He sent her a wink.

She shuddered at the very thought of a cave's close confines. "Food is staying in the very nice kitchen at the house, thank you very much." She still hadn't actually cooked in it, aside from sliding Zane's cinnamon rolls into the oven, which didn't count. Lunch had just been sandwiches and soup she'd had in the freezer. But tomorrow she intended to put it to full use.

"How much do you guys know about the cave systems around here?" Ryan looked at each of the locals in turn, brows lifted.

"Well, my son Ryder has explored some of them a good bit, thinking it was where our uncle got lost back in 1960." Uncle Gordon nodded toward Dad. Then Hannah. "Hannah could tell you more about that, I'm sure. But that cave wasn't near the Payne place or anything. I doubt they're connected. This area's just full of them."

"I've never heard of one out that way." Dad leaned forward a bit to ask Liam, "Have you?"

Liam shook his head. He'd been pretty quiet tonight, and Hannah wasn't sure if it was because he couldn't get a word in edgewise, if he enjoyed the storytelling from the crew, or something else. "No, nothing. I checked our records when Hannah told me about the call from Brooke Payne, and it doesn't look like we've ever been called to a cave in that area. We do occasionally help with rescues or investigate smoke spotted in a cave," he added to the couch crew.

Dad shrugged and rubbed Zeus's ears. "There could be a cave there, of course. Plenty of them around on private property that don't get explored much."

Ryan looked about to respond but paused when the theme song from *Raiders of the Lost Ark* burst into the room. It took Hannah a second to realize it was his ringtone. "Sorry, excuse me," he said, frowning as he pulled out the phone. "It's Ford Payne." He heaved himself up and headed for the kitchen as he answered. "Hello?"

In Ryan's absence, several different conversations started, all of them soft. Trevor and Lexi, Lacy and Neil. No doubt consulting as to when it would be time to head home. Dad set Zeus down and pushed himself up too, vanishing in the direction of the bathroom.

Hannah was usually still up and going strong at the Hot Spot at this time of night, but Liam yawned beside her. She angled a smile at him. "Long day?"

His fingers trailed lightly over her shoulder. "With a fantastic ending. Do you have to go back to the rental house for anything, or are you going home after this?"

"Home. I prepped everything at the rental before we left this afternoon. I'll probably pop into the restaurant first and make sure everything's good there, but I won't stay long. I have to be out earlier than usual in the morning." She was glad Dad had suggested the big group dinner. It had been fun to see her worlds combined. "You still good to help out tomorrow after work?"

"Barring an emergency, I'm there." He gave her the smile he reserved for her, the one that always made her feel warm and happy. Until it wobbled. "As long as you still need me, of course."

Her brows flew up. "Why wouldn't I?"

He shrugged, cast his gaze out to the group. "I don't know. There are a lot of hands you could recruit."

"Yeah, but they're the hands I'm being paid to supply with food, not recruit to help with it." Which sounded a bit weird, considering those hands belonged to friends too. "I mean, they'll have been working all day. I mean, *you* will have been too, so I get it if you're too tired."

"Hannah." Liam smiled again. "I volunteered to help because I want to spend time with you. I'm not trying to get out of it. I just don't want to be in the way."

"You won't be."

"Okay then." He looked like he was about to say more but fell silent when Ryan stepped back into the room.

"We have to go," Ryan told Kayla. "Apparently, the doorbell camera at the rental house sent Ford an alert a couple of minutes ago, but it was blurry, as if something was stuck in front of the lens. He was hoping we'd bumped it, but we haven't been there for hours. He's out of town this evening and can't check on it, so he needs us to."

Dad reemerged from the hallway but stood beside Lacy's chair rather than reclaim his spot on the love seat.

"I bet it's the key-stealing ghost." Oran hopped to his feet. "Let's go capture it on camera, *Uncover the Unknown* style. We can do a spin-off episode."

Kayla rolled her eyes and held out a hand toward Ryan, who obligingly helped her to her feet. "Not a ghost, Oran. But if we're dealing with an intruder of some kind, then we'd better go check it out."

Trevor and Lexi stood too, Lexi yawning. "Bet it's just a moth. That's happened to our doorbell camera before. They're attracted to the light."

"My money's on sneaky Phil." Ryan turned to Dad and Uncle Gordon. "Thank you guys for an amazing evening. Gordon, your fries are the bomb, and I would eat them every day of the week." He shook hands with her uncle, then moved to her father. "Gabriel, best burger ever. Seriously. It's easy to see where Hannah gets her skills."

Dad laughed. "Hardly. That's all from her mother. Good to meet you, Ryan. All of you."

Ryan had moved on to Lacy and Neil, who'd both stood as well. "Neil, my man, I need to come see this shop of yours. That map is awesome, and I need someone to geek out with about it."

"Come by anytime." Neil grinned, an arm around Lacy. "My fellow map geeks are always welcome."

"Lacy, I'll see you tomorrow, I assume?" At her nod, he turned to the love seat, hand outstretched. "Liam, always an honor to hang out with our fearless first responders, and so good to meet the guy who's stolen our girl's heart."

Hannah nearly rolled her eyes. It was one thing when Kayla called her "our girl" to Lacy. She and Kayla kept in touch. But Ryan?

She could count on one hand the exchanges they'd had since that one and only date, and none of them had been more than random comments on social media. But then, that was Ryan. He collected friends like Neil collected books, and much like Neil with books, cherishing them didn't necessarily mean frequent interactions in his mind. As long as when there was interaction, it was warm and friendly and sincere.

Liam shook Ryan's hand, smiling. "No stealing was involved, but I certainly am grateful she gave me such a gift. And it's always great to meet more of her friends."

Ryan held on to Liam's hand rather than releasing it, his smile nearly blinding. He looked at Hannah with wide eyes. "This guy is the real deal, isn't he? I hope so. We need to get coffee or something sometime, dude. I think I need a few lessons from you."

Not sure what to make of that comment, Hannah peered past Ryan to Kayla, who frowned at Ryan's back.

Liam nodded. "Sure. Coffee sounds great."

"Awesome. Hannah, I get why you moved home. Your family is the best." Rather than reach to shake, he held his hand out for a high-five, which she gave him. "See you in the morning, oh worker of culinary miracles. And remember—there is no such thing as bacon too many days in a row. Just sayin'."

"I have to agree with Ryan on that one," Liam said.

Hannah laughed, standing with Liam once the procession of crew had moved out of the way and given them room. "See you tomorrow, guys. Watch for deer on the drive. And if there's a ghostly home-invading prankster waiting for you, let us know."

"It's a moth," Lexi called over her shoulder. "Dollars to doughnuts."

"Ooh, who has doughnuts?" Oran asked.

Hannah lingered with Liam in the doorway between the living room and the kitchen while the TV crew reclaimed their belongings and Dad saw them out. Lacy and Neil made their exit next, Lacy exchanging hugs with the Prentisses and Liam. Hannah and Liam helped Dad and Uncle Gordon gather all the glasses and dessert plates and load them into the dishwasher, then Hannah figured she and Liam should get out of their hair too, so they could unwind before bed.

After bidding them farewell, she tucked her hand into Liam's and kept their pace slow as they walked to their cars in the driveway. "You were quiet tonight. You okay?"

"Sure." He gave her hand a reassuring squeeze. "I was just taking it all in. That group is something else. Quite the dynamic they have, isn't it?"

"Yeah." She had no problem agreeing to that. "When I knew them in LA, Kayla and Ryan and Oran had been working together for maybe a year or two, so they were friends with one another, but not as close as they are now. Now they're more like family."

Liam let go of her hand to wrap an arm around her. He dropped a kiss on top of her head. "It was fun to watch. Though I have to ask about Ryan and Kayla. Is there anything there?"

"Not that I know of." She mentally replayed the interactions she'd seen between them on this trip. Was that why Ryan had gone stiff when Kayla joked about Hannah's "handsome fire chief" boyfriend? And the way Kayla's gaze always tracked Ryan—could that be more than just doing her job and keeping the star of the show in her sights? Was it why none of those "perfectly fine" guys from Indiana had ignited any sparks?

Hannah blew out a breath. "That's a great question. I need to do some prying."

Liam chuckled and gave her a squeeze. "I bet even if they're both interested, they're hesitant to say anything. It would change their dynamic. And make things really awkward if it didn't work out, given the close proximity of their jobs. So pry carefully, I guess."

Hannah nodded. "Definitely a delicate balance. But if they could make each other happy, maybe it's worth risking." She turned, wrapped her arms around Liam's middle, and smiled up at him. "How could I not want that for them, happy as I am?"

"Could well be why I'm seeing it there too." He pressed a long, soft kiss to her lips. "I love you, Hannah."

"I love you too." She rested her head against his shoulder for a moment, breathing in the scent of his laundry detergent, his after-shave, just him.

Maybe Dad was right—she'd have loved to be going home *with* Liam, not leaving him to do so. If they were married, this would be the start of their evening.

But they both had enough going on right now. She wasn't about to bring up such a loaded subject. And besides, they didn't need to rush. She liked this part of their love story. The way her pulse skittered whenever he was near, how his kiss made her feel warm all over. The next step could come whenever it came.

The night's chill seeped in through her jacket, and when she shivered, Liam chuckled and urged her toward her car. "Hey, be careful in that cave tomorrow."

She paused with her hand halfway to the door and grimaced. "I'm the craft services. I will not be in the horrible, tight, claustrophobia-inducing cave, thank you very much."

He snorted. "Right. When are you not tagging along on any adventure?"

She wrinkled her nose. He knew her too well. "Maybe to the cave. Not in it."

Liam chuckled. "Just be careful. And have fun. I'll see you a little after five."

They said their goodbyes and climbed into their cars. After starting hers, Hannah took a moment to plug in her phone—the battery was low—and checked her messages while she was at it to make sure no one from the Hot Spot had texted. She hadn't heard any dings, but the laughter had been rather loud at several points that evening.

Nothing from her staff, but there was another message from Marshall, saying packages would be coming her way soon.

After sending an acknowledgment, Hannah put the Subaru into reverse, only then noticing that Liam hadn't left yet. She looked over at him, and he waved and reversed out of his spot. He must have been waiting to make sure she was all right. She was so blessed to be loved by such a thoughtful man.

The Hot Spot was still crowded when she pulled in at home, but a quick check-in proved that the team had it all in hand. She did a pass through the dining room to greet the customers, praised the team for their efforts, and then climbed the stairs to her apartment.

It was a little strange to be up there, getting ready for bed, while she could still hear the crowd down below. But it was nice too. Cozy, really, to hear echoes of laughter coming through the vents.

She brushed her teeth but then moved to her computer instead of bed. She wasn't tired enough to sleep yet. She pulled up her email, since she hadn't had time to check it that afternoon.

She saw mostly the usual things, but one subject line in particular caught her eye. A MESSAGE FOR YOUR HOLLYWOOD FRIENDS.

Her gaze tracked to the name, John Smith. "Okay, that's not weird or anything," she muttered. She opened it, bracing herself for something, though she wasn't sure what.

Two sentences was all that greeted her. Short, if not exactly sweet. No signature.

Tell your friends from Hollywood to butt out and let the past's secrets stay buried. That diamond isn't theirs to find.

Hannah stared at the message. She had a feeling that alert from the doorbell cam hadn't been a moth after all.

Chapter Ten

Kayla had been frowning most of the morning, and Hannah felt more than a little guilty to be the one to have inspired at least some of those scowls. Not that it was her fault that someone had sent her a mildly threatening email, but even so, she'd hated to greet her friend with it first thing in the morning.

At least the doorbell camera had been fine last night, and they'd found no evidence of anyone lurking about the house.

Currently, Kayla's knitted brows were directed at the weather app that was open on her laptop on the kitchen island. "I don't like the looks of that storm system." Heaving a sigh, she raised her eyes to where Ryan was pouring himself another cup of coffee. The crew had already eaten breakfast, and Hannah and Lacy took care of the dishes while Trevor, Lexi, and Oran attended to their own tasks. Only Ryan and Kayla lingered. "If this doesn't change, we're looking at almost a solid week of steady rain, starting tomorrow afternoon."

Ryan scowled. "I hate filming in the rain. I mean, we'll do it if we have to, but it's not ideal."

"It also depends on the cave. You know very well I'll pull the plug if any water is involved. You will not be repeating your adventure in that sea cave on the coast of Cornwall, Mr. Hall."

"Oh, I remember that one!" Lacy spun to face Ryan and Kayla, still drying the pan they'd used for hash browns. Her eyes were wide. "I seriously thought someone was about to die on camera. The way those waves bashed you into the rocks?" She shook her head.

Hannah was glad she hadn't caught whichever episode that was. Even knowing she probably would have heard if something serious had happened to her friends, it would have made her far too anxious to watch.

Ryan made a face. "Yeah. At the time, I thought it was an acceptable risk, but that was probably the closest we've ever come to death or serious injury while filming. We got out with barely minutes to spare before the cave filled at high tide. I thought Kayla was going to kill me when we got back to base."

Kayla closed her eyes. "I have never been so scared in my life. From my vantage point, I could see the water levels rising and the waves crashing at the mouth of the cave. Then half the crew was out, frantically shouting and pointing into the cave. But no Ryan or Trevor."

Ryan grinned. "Still, if I hadn't endangered the life of my camera operator, my sound engineer might never have charged up to him and kissed him senseless. I totally deserve the credit for that match made in heaven."

Kayla chuckled. "If you ever want to play matchmaker again, pick a way that doesn't involve nearly drowning, okay?" She checked her watch. "Brooke should be here by now."

"Well, her tardiness means that Hannah and Lacy will be able to join us." He sent a grin their way. "I couldn't have planned that better myself."

Hannah and Lacy exchanged smiles. Ryan and Kayla had indeed invited them to come along on the cave exploration. Hannah needed to prioritize her real job with the group, so she'd said it depended on if they got breakfast cleaned up in time—and that she had no intention of going into the cave itself. But she had some downtime before she needed to start lunch prep, and tagging along on part of the adventure sounded like a lot more fun than reviewing orders and invoices for the restaurant.

"I bet that's Brooke," Lacy said, peering out the window as she dried the last pot and handed it to Hannah to put away.

A Suburban rolled slowly up the bumpy driveway. Hannah hung the pot on its hook and peeked out the window again in time to see a pretty redhead—probably a decade or so younger than herself—hop out and jog toward the kitchen entrance.

Kayla was already at the door, holding it open for her with a smile. "Morning. Brooke?"

"That's me. Kayla?"

Kayla nodded and reached to shake the newcomer's hand as she stood aside to let her in. She made quick introductions. "Brooke, this is Ryan, Hannah, and Lacy."

Brooke didn't even glance at Hannah or Lacy. She was far too busy gushing over the hand Ryan held out to her, clinging to it with both of her own instead of shaking and letting go. "Oh my goodness, *Ryan Hall*! You're even taller than you look on camera. I'm a big fan of the show. I've watched them all, and *Uncover the Unknown* too. Between seasons I don't know what to do with myself on Wednesday nights. I've been dying to meet you for years and couldn't believe it when Dad said y'all were coming here to Blackberry Valley. I've always felt this kinship with you, you know? Like we were destined to be friends."

Kayla had closed the door and moved past Brooke and Ryan by then, which meant only Hannah and Lacy could see her roll her eyes. In a whisper, she told them, "This happens at least once on every trip these days."

Ryan extracted his hand from Brooke's and eased back a step as he said, "I'm always happy to make another friend. But I'm nothing more than the face of the show. It's Kayla who deserves most of the credit for making *Destination Discovery* so entertaining."

Hannah knew for a fact that they were a team and that Ryan did every bit as much work researching and making contacts, but she could appreciate how quick he was to share the credit. And Kayla certainly deserved her fair share of it. She'd been up for hours already by the time Hannah and Lacy had arrived these last two days, and from the sound of it, she was always the last to bed too. Never idle, even while the others took breaks.

"What he means is that I'm the taskmaster." Kayla grabbed her rain jacket from the back of a chair. "And it's time for me to crack the whip if we want to squeeze in as much as we can before the rain hits tomorrow. Ry, can you let the team know Brooke has arrived? And Brooke, I need you to sign the release form I emailed to you for review, and then we'll go outside and find a good spot to film the introduction." Her gaze flicked to Hannah and Lacy. "Can I strap wearable cameras to you two? Or if you'd rather be on camera, you can sign releases too."

They both laughed and said in unison, "Wearable cameras, please."

Five minutes later, they were all out in the spring sunshine. Brooke continued to fawn over Ryan, while Kayla gave the crew last-minute instructions and got Hannah and Lacy set up with small cameras. "You can either wear them or hold them," she said, screwing a rod to the bottom of one of the cameras and wiggling it around to show them how it stabilized itself.

"I'll hold mine," Hannah said, then accepted the one Kayla offered her.

"Me too," Lacy agreed.

Kayla attached the rod to the second camera too. "Great. Just keep them pointed at either Brooke or Ryan at all times. If the terrain gets rough and you need your hands, don't stop the recording. Tuck the camera into this harness and hang it around your neck." She handed them each a circular harness.

Hannah slipped hers on so the transition would be easier later if needed. She held the camera up on its stick and pointed it toward Ryan and Brooke. The younger woman clipped a mic pack onto the back waistband of her pants, while Lexi showed her how to hide the mic under her shirt.

Kayla started the recording on Hannah's and Lacy's cameras, then her own. She put hers into its harness before she handled the clapboard to kick off the day's production.

Ryan hopped a few steps away from Brooke for the walk-up, the handshake, and quick intro. Then he asked, "So did you grow up on this property?"

Brooke had obviously dressed with the intention of being on camera. Why she'd chosen white pants for a hike through the countryside, Hannah couldn't guess, but the woman's army-green blouse certainly coordinated well with Ryan's signature khaki button-down. A coincidence? Hannah didn't think so.

The younger woman smiled and tucked a long lock of hair behind her ear. "No, but—"

"Hold up," Lexi called out. When everyone looked at her, she offered Brooke a smile. "Sorry. Brooke, could you take off your necklace and bracelets? They jangle every time you move, and mess with the audio."

Brooke scowled. "But they draw the outfit together."

Lexi's smile tightened. "Yes, and they're very pretty. But also very loud. Sorry."

"You'll still look great without them," Ryan assured her.

With a huff, Brooke unfastened her necklace, slipped off the stack of bangles she wore, and pouted at Lexi. "What am I supposed to do with them?"

Kayla jogged forward. "I'll put them in my bag. Thanks, Brooke." She secured the items in the front pouch of her bag and then turned to face the cameras. "Take the greeting from the top."

They did, Ryan repeating his question about Brooke growing up there.

Brooke smiled. "I grew up about a mile down the road, so I was here a lot, visiting my grandfather. I ran all over the area with my cousins. That's how we discovered the cave."

"Can you tell me about this cave?" Ryan asked.

"I can do better than that, Ryan. I can show you."

"Even better." He grinned. "Lead the way."

Brooke turned to the northwest, and the whole crew fell into step behind her. Kayla had already coached her to be sure to present at least her profile to the camera before speaking, and Hannah had to give her credit for obeying those instructions to a T. She seemed perfectly aware of where the cameras were as they strode through the field.

"My cousins and I found the cave when I was about eleven," she said. "At first we thought it was nothing more than a crack in the rock. We always loved finding good places for hide-and-seek. We decided to see how deep it went and if the shadows could hide us. But after several steps downward, it opened up into an honest-to-goodness cave, with several chambers and even a place where a spring makes a little pool."

"Water," Kayla muttered under her breath. "Great."

"And what makes you think this cave was the hiding place of our mysterious outlaw?" Ryan asked.

Brooke gave him a cheeky grin. "The things we found *in* the cave, of course."

"What things?" Ryan pressed, echoing the question in Hannah's mind.

Her grin only grew. "You'll see."

Kayla jogged a few steps forward. "Okay, stop for a minute." They'd reached the edge of the woods, and the group halted at the start of a deer trail. "Brooke, how rugged is the terrain for this part?"

"Not too bad," Brooke assured her. "There's a small incline, and then we'll have to cross a creek, but there are bits of submerged wood we can use as stepping stones."

Kayla pursed her lips, then said, "Okay, let's plan on running the path at least twice. Trevor, you'll take point and get the approaching shots. Oran, the back view. Then we'll reshoot from Ryan's POV. Brooke, can you show the path to Trevor so he can find the best locations for his shots?"

Brooke huffed a breath. "Can't we just go?"

Kayla arched her brows. "Welcome to the film world. Every second you see on your screen has been selected from about twenty possible seconds. Everything is done at least twice, more often three to five times. We need multiple camera angles of everyone, not to mention immersive ones to make the viewer feel like they're with us." She flashed a too-sweet grin. "But I'm sure being part of it will give you an even deeper appreciation for Ryan and all his hard work."

Ryan shot her a playful glare.

Brooke refreshed her smile and said, "Of course," even though she obviously wasn't any too pleased.

Hannah leaned close to Lacy. "I think we made the right call in not pursuing show biz like we dreamed of when we were ten."

"You can say that again." Lacy rubbed her stomach. "Did you bring any granola bars or anything? I'm somehow hungry again already."

Hannah reached into her cross-body bag and pulled out one of the snacks she'd packed. She had decided that if she tagged along, she might as well continue to do her job. Especially since craft services usually provided snack foods on set. She had several water bottles, energy bars, and a couple of apples in the bag. "Here you go, Mama."

A full hour passed before they finally finished filming the passage across the small creek and arrived at the opening in the rocks that Brooke had described. Their guide checked her hair and got into position by the opening, flashing a smile at Oran. "I'm ready whenever you guys are."

"Wait a minute." Kayla had said that phrase more times than Hannah could count in the last hour, every time Brooke tried to push forward when Kayla wanted them to backtrack for a third or fourth take from a different angle.

Brooke made no effort to control the roll of her eyes.

For that matter, neither did Ryan, though his eye roll was for the crew's benefit, not at their expense. "What's up, Kay?"

Kayla pulled out her phone and brought up the map feature. She dropped a pin on their current location and did something Hannah couldn't make sense of, then shook her head. "Didn't your dad say the current property is only five acres?"

Brooke frowned. "Yeah. So?"

"So there's no way we're on Payne property anymore. Unless you own this tract?"

Brooke went stiff. "No."

Kayla drew in a long breath and put on what Hannah had come to learn was her professional smile. "Another family member?"

A shake of the head sent Brooke's careful curls swaying.

Ryan, still facing the crew rather than their guide, squeezed his eyes shut and mouthed counting to ten before spinning around. "Do you know who owns the property?"

Brooke shrugged. "No idea. It doesn't matter. We all come and go however we like around here. No one cares."

"Oh boy," Lacy muttered to Hannah.

Kayla kept her professional smile in place. "I'm sure that's true when it comes to hiking and exploring, but things get complicated when you introduce film. We have to obey strict guidelines, or our network could refuse to air the episode. Liability is alive and well in our industry. We have strict instructions not to do any guerilla film work."

Brooke wrinkled her nose. "What does this have to do with gorillas?"

"Guerrilla, not gorilla," Ryan corrected, his voice easy and light. "You know, like guerilla warfare? When you film without permission or the proper release forms signed, that's what it's called. Indie filmmakers can get away with it sometimes, but we can't, or we all lose our jobs."

Brooke scoffed. "That's ridiculous."

Kayla looked as though she was barely keeping her temper. "Okay. Change of plans. Oran and Trevor and Lexi, feel free to scout around for more great angles, but no more filming until I can track down the owner. For which I would really like my computer instead of my phone, so I'm headed to the house."

Ryan strode away from the cave opening. "I'm with you."

Brooke folded her arms over her chest. "So what does this mean? You get permission and we come back this afternoon?"

"We can hope, but it's more likely to be another day." Kayla slid her phone into her pocket and picked up the clapboard she'd leaned against a tree. "Let's try to get it sorted by tomorrow, or we'll run out of good weather. Because we are not filming in a cave with a water source when it's pouring down rain."

"Why? It'll be totally fine. It's a little pool," Brooke said.

Kayla's face lost all hint of her professional smile. "Not your call."

Ryan slid an arm around Kayla's shoulders and led her back toward the path. "No caves in the rain. We're agreed. We'll work it all out somehow, Kayla, like we always do."

Hannah turned with Lacy to fall in behind Kayla and Ryan as the crew scattered. She looked over her shoulder and saw Brooke finally trudging after them.

"Another day doesn't work," the young woman whined. "I could only get today off, and my boss said I'd be fired if I took any more time. I'm out of personal days and vacation time for the year."

Already? It was only April. Hannah reminded herself that she shouldn't judge others, especially when she didn't know their stories. For all she knew, Brooke had been sick a lot, or taken time off to help someone else who was, or to go on a mission trip for something. She had no way of knowing and wasn't about to ask.

"I'll do my best to get permission ASAP. But if we have to shoot another day, we'll either have to do it without a local guide, or with different ones." Kayla flashed a conspiratorial smile at Hannah and Lacy. "You two will be available, right? You're locals. And Hannah, you did some caving with your cousin, so you know enough of the lingo. I know you don't want to go in, but you could lead us to it."

Lacy grinned, no doubt in response to the huff of annoyance from behind them. Hannah almost wanted to take pity on Brooke and promise not to hog the spotlight, but she couldn't refuse to help her friends. This snag wasn't their fault. Hannah had read Brooke's email after her initial phone call with Kayla, and she had definitely made it sound like the cave was on Payne property.

Hannah gave her friends a smile. "You know I'll do whatever I can to help. Though if that means we're relegated to takeout at any point, it's your own fault."

Kayla and Ryan both laughed.

Ryan's arm finally slid away from Kayla's shoulder when they had to clamber over a downed branch. "If that happens, we'll just go to the Hot Spot again. I'm not worried. In fact, I'll take any excuse to eat at your place again, Hannah. Your whole family has incredible culinary gifts."

Kayla invited Brooke inside when they got back to the house. Hannah, hoping to smooth ruffled feathers, made sure to offer Brooke whatever she might like from the snack table. She brought the charcuterie board from the fridge and slid it into place, then set about lunch prep. She had the time now, even though it was still a little early.

Kayla's laptop was plugged into one of the outlets at the island, and she wasted no time getting to work. Hannah didn't bother trying to follow what she was doing, but it involved many browser tabs and a lot of clicking and typing.

"Taco bar for lunch today, right?" Lacy asked.

Hannah nodded. "I haven't had a chance to prep the veggies yet, so if you'd be willing to shred the lettuce or dice the tomatoes, that would be great. I'm going to work on the meat." She had traditional ground beef, some steak chunks, and chicken she'd put in a marinade that morning—a very different flavor profile from the chicken still marinating for dinner.

Ryan must have disappeared into his room with whatever task Kayla had given him, because when Hannah passed by the living room an hour later, she saw Brooke lounging alone on the couch. She stared idly at her cell phone, occasionally scrolling with her thumb.

"Can I get you anything, Brooke?"

The younger woman raised her head without a smile. "No."

Hannah chose not to take the rudeness personally. "All right. I'll be in the kitchen if that changes." Upon reentering her domain, Hannah nudged Kayla to get her attention from her laptop. "Need anything, Kay?"

Her friend tossed her a grin, though her eyes didn't really seem to focus on Hannah. "I'm good, though a bit tortured from the smells of whatever you're cooking. I'm in favor of an early lunch today if that's possible."

"Kinda thought that might be the idea, in case you need to go back out this afternoon. Any luck on the property stuff?"

"Sort of." Kayla reached for the coffee mug she'd left beside her laptop that morning, then scowled into it. "I've tracked it to a Cody Coleman, but I haven't found contact info for him yet."

"Cody Coleman," Hannah repeated, brows drawing together as she tried to place the name. "Sounds familiar. Do you know any Colemans, Lacy?"

Lacy looked up from the tomatoes she was dicing. "Not sure. It does sound familiar, but I don't think I know him on a personal level."

With a shake of her head, Hannah got back to work, knowing her mind sometimes found answers more readily when her hands were busy. Sure enough, a few minutes later, it came to her. "I know why it sounds familiar. He has a band."

Lacy sent a questioning look her way. "Have you heard them play?"

"No. But about a month ago he stopped in to ask if we did live music. I told him it wasn't part of the current plan, but he left me with a demo track and his business card in case I changed my mind."

Kayla let out a long hum. "I typed in 'Blackberry Valley,' 'Cody Coleman,' and 'band,' and the first link leads me to a website under construction. No contact information."

"He told me they were looking for someone to build their website, so I'm not surprised," Hannah said. "I can run to town after lunch and grab his card. I just stuck it in my desk drawer." She hadn't listened to the demo he'd given her, since she really had no plans to introduce live music, but one lesson she'd learned from Ryan long ago was to never throw out someone's contact info. There was no telling when it might come in handy, and this was a perfect example.

"That would be awesome." Kayla glanced toward the door to the hallway. "I'll go see if Brooke knows him. Maybe that should have been my first step, given that they're obviously neighbors."

Hannah just smiled, not needing to ask why that hadn't been her first step. When Ryan wasn't in the room, Brooke's attitude was anything but open and generous.

And she must not have had any useful information, because Kayla returned to the kitchen two minutes later with a distinctly irritated look on her face. "I guess we're relying on you unearthing that business card, Hannah. Brooke doesn't know 'every person who comes to the area and buys up property intending to flip houses or drive up the market price of land.'" She made air quotes with her fingers. "And she seemed far more interested in whether Ryan and I are 'a thing' rather than actually helping with the show." Kayla scowled.

Hannah winked. Here was her opening. "And? Are you? He did have his arm around you an awful lot this morning."

Kayla rolled her eyes, but was that a bit of disappointment in them, or just Hannah's imagination? "You know Ryan. He's affectionate with all his friends, and he especially likes to play that up to discourage a particular sort of fan." Her lips quirked into a smile. "He had us all but engaged last year when this woman kept throwing herself at him, promising funding for the show if he'd just 'take some time to tell her about it.'" Her voice went low and breathy, and she batted her eyes dramatically.

Hannah and Lacy both burst into laughter. Hannah might have pressed the real question if they were alone, but she knew that Kayla wouldn't unburden her heart with anyone else around—or when Ryan could walk in on the conversation at any moment.

Their laughter had no sooner faded than a phone rang down the hall, and seconds later Brooke's voice came from the living room. "Hey, Dad."

Hannah, Lacy, and Kayla all returned to their tasks. Hannah wasn't trying to listen, but Brooke made no attempt to lower her voice.

"No, I'm not 'bothering' the film crew. I'm at work." A pause stretched for a few seconds. "Well, if you saw my car here and already knew, why did you ask?"

At that, Kayla looked up from her computer, gaze catching on Hannah's. Brooke's call and email to them yesterday had also sounded like she'd reached out at her father's request, but they'd wondered about that, given his warning. And she wondered more now.

"No, Dad. No, I—will you just listen?" Her voice went muffled, though by no means difficult to hear. "I'm answering their questions and showing them some things in the woods I found as a kid. Relax." Another beat, and then, "Yes, *fine*. And yes, I'll be back at work tomorrow. No, I just took the day. I had the day left! I'm not making a liar out of you with your friend. I *am* a good worker." Brooke sounded ready to growl, and she'd gotten louder with each sentence. "Fine. Bye."

Kayla made a show of fastening her eyes on her computer screen as footsteps stomped their way. Lacy cut the tomatoes with more attention than the task required, and Hannah couldn't blame her. She was arranging soft tortillas on a plate with unprecedented studiousness too.

"Any luck tracking down this Coleman guy?" Brooke asked as she entered.

Kayla didn't look up from whatever she was typing. "Hannah has his contact information at home. She's going to go get it after lunch."

Brooke tossed Hannah a scorching glare. "Why doesn't Hannah go now, so we can get back out there this afternoon?"

Hannah forced a smile. "Because I need to get lunch ready, since that's my primary job. But I'll go as soon as I have the food out."

Kayla raised an eyebrow at her. "No, you'll eat first, while it's hot. Twenty minutes won't make that big a difference."

Brooke clearly disagreed, but since she wasn't the boss, Hannah ignored her. She turned to the drawer she had put her utensils in— and halted, staring. She'd just put the ones they'd used for breakfast away before they went out, but now the drawer was empty.

Their prankster was clearly still around.

Chapter Eleven

***

Friday morning dawned warmer but cloudy, giving credence to the forecast that still predicted a solid week of rain beginning that afternoon.

Hannah put the last of the breakfast dishes away at the rental house and lunged for her phone when it rang. When she saw the number on the screen with *Cody Coleman* above it, she called, "It's him. He's finally returning my call."

She'd left Cody a message the day before right after lunch, but until he got in touch, they were at a standstill. The crew had breathed a sigh of relief when Brooke declared the day a waste and left around two o'clock. They then spent the whole afternoon and evening doing research and B-roll. Kayla promised to call Brooke if they heard from Cody with permission that afternoon, but Hannah suspected no one was sad that he'd missed that window.

She had spent an inordinate amount of time looking for her missing utensils, finally finding them stashed in a box in the pantry. That pointed to the move being intentional, but the crew all claimed ignorance, and Hannah was inclined to believe them. They seemed as baffled by the prank as she was. She explained the incident to Liam when he arrived, but he didn't have any ideas either. He cautioned them to be careful and double-check the locks whenever they left the house.

Now she swiped to accept the call and tried to modulate her voice as she said, "Hello?"

"Hi, Hannah. It's Cody. Sorry, I just got your message. I have to say when I saw your number, that wasn't the request I was expecting."

He sounded amused, which was in line with her impression of him when they'd met nearly a year before. She remembered a guy who was energetic and full of ideas. He'd said something about having moved to the area recently, which explained the clipped accent that put her in mind of New England, though she wasn't sure which region. "Hi, Cody. And yeah, I bet. Did my message make sense though?"

She'd tried to be concise yet give all the relevant details, but she was no Kayla.

"Oh, sure. And I'm totally cool with granting permission. How do I go about doing that?"

Some of the anxiety from the last twenty-four hours evaporated at those words. She was wondering what they'd do if permission didn't come through. It would have meant they couldn't check out the cave, and might have killed the episode altogether. Their only hope would be that some other information would come to light that would make decent television.

Fortunately, none of that seemed to be happening. "Great question. I'm going to hand you to Kayla for that. She's the one in charge over here. I just called because I had your number."

"Cool. Is she around?"

"Yep. Here she is now." Hannah passed the phone to Kayla, who had set up her base of operations at the island that morning.

Kayla's professional tone and smile were in full force. "Mr. Coleman, I'm Kayla Dreher, producer of *Destination Discovery*."

She gave him a quick rundown of the situation, explained exactly where the cave was, and agreed that a digital signature would be fine. She promised to email a form to him right away.

By the time she said goodbye and handed Hannah's phone to her, she was doing a little jig. "Yes, yes, yes! I love it when people are easy to work with." She leaned over her laptop, clicked a few times, then said, "Form sent, and he promised he'd be watching for it to come in and would get it back to us pronto."

While they waited for the return email, the crew gathered their gear—more than yesterday. Hannah paused while reaching for her rain jacket when Oran dumped an enormous bag in front of the door. "What's that?"

Oran smiled at her. "Caving gear. When we thought the cave was on this property, we planned on coming back for it if we needed it. But it's far enough away that it makes more sense to haul it with us from the get-go. It's got flashlights, headlamps, rope, rappelling equipment—anything we're likely to need in a cave."

That made sense, though the very thought of why they'd *need* all those lights and ropes made her chest go tight. And rappelling? Brooke hadn't mentioned any big drops. Then again, she hadn't proved herself to be the most accurate source of information.

"Actually, Oran, if you wanted to go ahead and run that to the cave and then come back for your camera, that might make the most sense." Kayla clicked the refresh button on her browser again.

"I'm on it, boss." He slid his jacket on, tied his boots, and then hefted the duffel over his shoulder.

Trevor strode to the outlet behind the table where they'd plugged in their rechargeable batteries—or some of them, anyway. Hannah had seen the charging stations all over the house. "You've got to be kidding me. Who unplugged the batteries?"

Everyone in the kitchen spun toward Trevor with wide eyes, making it clear this was an unspeakable horror. Hannah had to exchange a look with Lacy. They were, after all, the most likely suspects, given that the kitchen was their domain, but they both shook their heads. "Wasn't us," Hannah said. "I know better than to touch a film crew's batteries."

"And I'm not crawling over that bench to get to that plug unless I'm chasing a stray chocolate bar." Lacy rested her hand on her stomach.

"Plug them back in," Kayla said with a sigh. "Did the other sets charge?"

"I think so. They were still plugged in, anyway."

"Then we'll hope we have enough without this set. If we don't, I'll run back to get these later. They should be good by the time we'd need them."

"Assuming the plug doesn't mysteriously fall out of the outlet again," Lexi muttered. "If I didn't know better, I might start to think Oran's onto something with this ghost theory. You know what was missing last night? My *toothbrush*. Who steals a girl's toothbrush?"

Kayla frowned. "You didn't tell me that."

"That's because I found it in the bedside table drawer." Lexi folded her arms over her chest. "Don't much like the idea that someone was in our room though."

Trevor, having plugged the charger back in, moved around the table again and rubbed his wife's shoulder. "I don't like it either. But it's been harmless stuff. Someone's just taking up Phil's prankster ways. Probably Oran."

Hannah didn't think that fit with Oran's personality, but it had been years since she'd hung out with him, and she had no idea what influence Phil might have had. Maybe he *was* playing pranks to line up with his ghost theory, to pay his friends back for their mocking him about it. It kind of made sense. He could have done all the things—well, aside from the alert from the doorbell camera, but that could have really just been a moth.

"There's Cody's signed form." Kayla pumped a fist in the air and closed her laptop. "Okay, everyone gather anything you don't want disappearing and put it in your bedroom and lock the door. All the rooms have keys, right?"

At her friends' nods, Kayla unplugged her power cord. "Actually, I'll take those batteries to my room, since I'll be the one coming back for them if necessary. Trev, will you grab them for me?" Kayla grimaced at Hannah while Trevor once again climbed over the long bench on the far side of the table. "I don't know what to tell you, Hannah. We can't exactly lock up all the kitchen equipment."

Hannah shrugged. "If this prankster wants to eat, they'll leave my stuff alone." The missing utensils had been annoying, but it hadn't actually hindered her meal prep.

Kayla laughed. "Good point. All right, I'll be right back. Meet you all outside."

Lexi ran upstairs to lock their bedroom. Hannah heard her conveying Kayla's advice to Ryan when she met him in the hall. Hannah and Lacy did a final check of everything in the kitchen, shrugged into their jackets, and headed outside.

Kayla joined them a few minutes later, the last to arrive, flipping stapled pages until she found whatever she was looking for. "Okay.

Let's refilm the whole scene we did yesterday, but with Hannah and Lacy standing in as our local guides."

"What?" Hannah asked, startled. "I thought you wanted to film us right outside the cave. We can't exactly claim we have any personal history with this place."

"Don't have to." Kayla didn't even look up. "We'll tell the story however we need to. You can claim to be a local who has heard about this cave—which you have. We don't have to say it's only been in the last two days. Then you lead the way, and we explore together, with you telling the story Brooke told us, since she's not here to do it. You don't have to say it's *your* story."

Hannah glanced to Ryan for help, but he shrugged. "This stuff happens all the time. It's best to have options and cover all our bases—and Brooke definitely struck me as the type to try to make things difficult since she couldn't see it through. Might be most efficient to cut her out completely. But we'll film the arrival at the cave both ways, with you two being our main guides *and* as if you showed up after Brooke delivered us there. We'll see which we like better in edits."

"Movie magic, I guess." Lacy made a show of fluffing her auburn hair. "How do I look?" They'd already done their makeup under Kayla's watchful eye.

"Ready for prime time." Ryan gave Lacy's shoulder an encouraging pat and then pulled a radio from his belt and keyed it on. "How's it going, Oran? Over."

A few seconds passed, then the radio squawked to life. "Five minutes out. I stashed the gear inside the opening of the cave so it wouldn't be in our shots until we're ready for it. Over."

Kayla moved closer to Hannah and Lacy. "Since we're filming you guys, no cameras for you today. You get wireless mics instead." She held out small rectangles with clips. "Body pack. Just hook it to your waistband, then feed the wire up under your shirt and clip the mic out of sight somewhere in the front."

Hannah and Lacy obeyed, then presented themselves to Kayla for inspection.

Kayla went behind each of them, clicked something, and then helped them cover the pack with their shirt. "There, they're on. Now you can forget about it. It's in Lexi's hands. She'll let you know if she's getting too much noise from clothing or anything. Just be your usual friendly selves. Add any local lore you know that could be relevant. Lacy, feel free to mention that your husband provided us with our maps. And don't look at the camera."

Hannah nodded. "Only Ryan gets to do that."

Kayla grinned. "That's right. You get to talk to him, and he gets to talk to the audience. Here." She reached up and smoothed Hannah's hair. "There you go. Perfect."

Hannah passed the bag with the food and water to her. "Guessing you'd rather not have this in the shot?"

"Good guess." Kayla slung it over her head, in the opposite direction of her own bag. She also had a backpack on and the camera harness around her neck. She appeared ready for a serious expedition into something more intimidating than the little forest between there and the cave. "Nervous?"

Hannah and Lacy exchanged a glance. "A little," Hannah admitted. "But not about the cameras as much as the cave. They're not my favorite places."

"I'm fine with the cave, but the camera thing is freaking me out," Lacy said.

"Hannah, you can stay outside the cave with Kayla if you want. And Lacy, you'll be great." Ryan clipped the radio onto his belt and covered it with his usual khaki shirt. How many of those did he own, anyway? "Want to practice before Oran gets back?"

Lacy nodded, so Kayla and Ryan closed the circle, Kayla taking the lead, as usual. "We'll probably do a voice-over as we have Ryan walking up to you guys. Something about how he's meeting up with two amazing locals, et cetera."

Ryan held out a hand and beamed at Hannah as if she were a complete stranger he'd been looking forward to meeting. "Hannah, hello! Thank you so much for coming out today. And this is Lacy, right?"

Lacy shook his hand too. "That's right."

"Now, correct me if I'm wrong, but isn't your husband the one who supplied us with our local maps?"

Lacy smiled. "Yes, that's right. My husband owns Legend & Key, a bookstore with the largest collection of maps in Kentucky." She shook her head. "I don't actually know if that's true, but Neil claims it."

Kayla laughed. "Just add 'one of the' to the phrase, and then I won't have to fact-check it."

"Works for me."

Ryan angled back toward Hannah. "And Hannah, you have some experience with local caves, is that right?"

Though her instinct was to downplay it—really, her cousin Ryder was the real expert—Hannah restrained herself. That wouldn't help the show. So she tilted her head and smiled. "A little, though I usually avoid going in them whenever possible."

"What can you tell us about the cave we're heading to today?"

She had to hand it to him. He knew how to phrase things so that she could share the story Brooke had told them without ever claiming it was *her* family story, or something she'd ever looked into before the last couple of days.

Once she'd finished recounting Brooke's tale, complete with the promise that they'd have to see for themselves what was in the cave, Ryan clapped. "See? You guys are awesome. And there's Oran, so let's gear up."

Glad they'd taken the time to run through it, Hannah gave her shoulders a roll to loosen them, reminding herself she didn't have to go in the cave if she didn't want to. Still, she admitted to herself that she was curious. As for the cameras, it was easy to ignore them, and she knew for a fact the focus would be on Ryan and his animated reactions rather than on her.

She and Lacy delivered their lines without any trouble, neither of them forgetting and accidentally looking at the cameras.

"Got it!" Kayla called cheerfully. "Great job, guys. I don't think we need another take, since we have Brooke's version too, but I'll review everything tonight and let you know if we need to reshoot. For now, let's get moving. The rain will be here before we know it."

The crew hurried to the spots they'd already marked out for themselves. Hannah, Lacy, and Ryan hiked along the path, past the cameras, then paused while the cameras were repositioned. Kayla didn't make them backtrack as often this time, saying they'd take shots from yesterday that only had Ryan in them to fill out the cut.

Now it made sense why Ryan wore the same shirt every day. He wore his signature hat too, which covered any differences in his hair from day to day. Another thing that Hannah had once found strange, but which now seemed logical.

They arrived at the cave faster than they had the day before. "I'll just add a voice-over about how storms began rolling in, to account for the changes in lighting," Ryan said. He got into the position by the mouth of the cave that he'd taken up yesterday with Brooke. Hannah and Lacy stood beside him.

Kayla clapped them in with her slate, they did the five-count of silence, and then Ryan flashed his camera-worthy grin. "Okay, so this is it?"

"This is it, Ryan," Hannah said, nodding.

He made a show of peering behind him. "You sure? Because this does not look like a cave opening—and I've been in a lot of caves."

Hannah and Lacy laughed, and Lacy said, "It may look like a simple crack in the rock face, but I promise, it opens up into a multi-chamber cave."

"And in that cave we'll find…?" He gave them the sort of smile that at once invited answers yet knew he wouldn't get them.

He made it easy to play off him. Hannah gave a playful shake of her head. "Oh no, we're not going to ruin the surprise. You need to get in there and see for yourself."

He glanced at the crack again, then turned to the camera. "I think I should have started that diet I keep meaning to try."

"Great." Kayla hiked the last few feet to where they stood. "Okay, now let's refilm as if Brooke has left us and Hannah and Lacy have arrived."

Once again, Ryan gave them the lead-in to make it easy to deliver the words with that slant, and soon Kayla flashed a thumbs-up.

"Perfect," she said, smiling. "Let's gear up, cameras ready for the montage." She turned to Hannah and Lacy. "Don't worry about noise. This part will have a voice-over."

They moved out of the way as Ryan retrieved the duffel bag Oran had stashed. Unzipping it revealed the treasure trove Oran had prepared. Ryan passed around headlamps and flashlights and pulled out some kind of handheld device.

Hannah debated a moment, pulling her bottom lip between her teeth. She didn't want to go into that cave, but she also really wanted to be part of the exploration. *Lord, could You lend me some strength?* Deciding to act on the prayer, she drew in a deep breath and held out a hand for a flashlight. "Okay, I'm not going to be left out. But what's that?" Hannah pointed to the device.

"Gas detector, to make sure the air inside is breathable," Ryan explained. "I don't expect a problem with this one, but you never know."

And now she was rethinking her decision.

Ryan didn't seem to notice. "Let me go in with this to make sure it's safe, then Trevor will go in to film us coming in."

"I never stopped to think about that," Lacy said to Hannah. "That the camera operators actually have to get in there first to record all the tricky climbs and descents and wriggling into tight places."

"Ryan has the glamorous job," Kayla said, coming to stand at Lacy's other side. "But the crew makes or breaks a show like this, and we've got the best. Trevor's actually a skilled rock climber and extreme sports enthusiast, which means if he needs a good shot he doesn't hesitate to do things most people wouldn't even think about doing. Oran can always find the perfect perspective thanks to his years in art school. Lexi trained with an orchestra before she took a summer gig on the equipment and discovered that her ear for music gives her a great ear for sound engineering too."

Lexi, still fiddling with her knobs and dials, said, "And Kayla is our Type A Organizer Extraordinaire with no equal in the known world."

Kayla chuckled. "Also known as oldest of five siblings. I went to film school but quickly realized it wasn't the writing or camerawork I love so much as the process."

Ryan squeezed back through the crack. "Fair warning, the entrance is a downward slope and will be slick once it starts raining. Air seems fine, and I only scraped a few body parts off, squeezing through there. I don't need a nose, right?"

"Noses are totally overrated." Kayla moved to the side again. "Okay, let's move, people. I'll be out here monitoring the weather, but don't waste a minute." She paused to look at Hannah. "You sure you're okay going in? Don't feel obligated."

Hannah's smile felt only a little shaky. "Best way to overcome a fear is to face it, right? Or something like that."

Kayla gave her an encouraging pat on the shoulder. "If it's too much, just come back out. No worries on our end. Lacy can be the in-the-cave guide if necessary."

Hannah and Lacy crouched down with Ryan to pull more items from the bag, letting Trevor and Oran get what shots they needed. Trevor then disappeared into the crevice, holding his camera over his head to keep from scraping it against the walls. He wore a bag that held battery-operated lights he would place around the cave to help cut the darkness.

"I'm in," he called out to them. "Give me a minute to find a good place and get some of these lights set up."

Once Trevor gave them the go-ahead, Ryan led the way inside. Lacy motioned for Hannah to go next, so she followed, quickly understanding Ryan's comment about the closeness and the slope. She could fit easily enough, but that didn't stop the feeling that the whole world was closing in on her. If she leaned forward or back even a little, the rock wall greeted her. And several times, her boot slipped on the damp rocks and she slid a few inches downward. She had to make a concerted effort to regulate her breathing.

Ryan's "No *way!*" told her when he'd reached the opening. He laughed, and she could imagine him gazing around with wonder. "This place is amazing! Look how big it is in here."

Big sounded good. She increased her pace and stepped into the cavern, which was big enough to ease the tightness in her chest. *Just a room*, she told herself. *A room made of rock.*

Trevor kept his camera on Ryan, but Hannah knew Oran would do a pan once he got inside to capture the scope of this first chamber. It was nothing like Mammoth Cave or some of the other big ones around, but it was definitely bigger than she would have guessed from surveying the opening and the surrounding area. She kept herself from exclaiming in surprise, since she was supposed to be the local expert.

Ryan moved into the cavern enough for Hannah and Lacy to come up beside him. "All right," he said to them, smile in place.

"Now comes the interesting part of the story, right? Let's see if we can find evidence that this is where Franklin Sullivan stayed. Ladies, lead the way."

He held out an arm to the right, so that was the direction Hannah went. She walked a few steps and then turned around. "You're going to come and actually take the lead now, right, Ryan? I have no idea where I'm going."

He laughed. "Yeah, let's explore a bit and then decide where we want to bring the audience. Brooke said this cave system only has a couple of rooms, but we'll see. Hopefully she's right."

Their headlamps didn't reach to the opposite wall of the main room, but they moved along the edge until an opening appeared on the right, and followed that in. Within a few steps, however, they splashed through water, and a gushing sound came from up ahead.

"Yeah." Ryan's voice echoed back to them. "Let's be glad Kayla stayed outside for this one."

Chapter Twelve

The Payne Farm
April 13, 1910

Elinor checked over her shoulder once more to be sure nothing stirred in the forest aside from birds and squirrels. She stilled the way Tom had taught her, holding the position long enough for the animals to get used to her and start their chirruping and squabbling again. Minutes that she used to pour out her heart, her fears, her hopes, her questions to God.

She still wasn't sure she was doing the right thing. But it was the only thing she could do. Last night she'd lain awake again, wondering if she should have told Nathan Davis about Franklin's visit. But every time she considered going into town to leave him a message, the same verse kept echoing in her mind. *A friend loveth at all times, and a brother is born for adversity.*

Franklin had always been that friend who loved her unconditionally, the brother she knew she could turn to with any trouble she found herself in. He was the one she'd confided in at age five when a bully down the street kept pushing her around and stealing her lunch. He was the one she knew she could trust with her first heartbreak at fourteen. He was the one she'd gone to for advice when she got into an argument with her best friend and didn't know how to reconcile with her.

He told her once that there was no mistake she could ever make, no sin she could commit, no offense she could give that would make him love her any less. He'd sworn that no matter what, he would be her champion. He would take care of her. He would love her through the storm.

How could she do any less for him?

The birds twittered, and the squirrels scolded them. A deer walked toward the stream. Satisfied that she was the only human out there, she edged into the cave's opening, her bag of supplies tight against her. Once inside, she called out, so she wouldn't startle him. "Franklin? It's Ellie."

She waited in the main chamber to see where an answer might come from while she fumbled for the electric flashlight she'd slipped into her bag. Tom had preferred the thing to a lantern whenever he was out in the barn, and she could see how it was safer around dry hay. But it ate through expensive batteries like Judah through cake, so she didn't use it often.

It was handy now though. If anyone had seen her this morning, they wouldn't have known she carried her light in her bag, so they wouldn't have wondered why. A lantern in her hand during the day might have sparked questions.

She switched the flashlight on and watched the beam slice through the darkness. Funny how accustomed she'd grown to living without electric lights—they were everywhere in Chicago and had been for decades. But no lines had been run to her house yet, and there was no telling when that might change. "Franklin?"

A rustling came from the left. "Ellie?"

She aimed the beam that way, making her brother wince against the onslaught and lift a hand to block his eyes. "Sorry." She lowered the light to shine on his knees and hurried toward him. "How are you doing?"

"Not bad, all things considered." He waved her into the chamber. It was much smaller than the main one, and warmer by a few degrees. He didn't have a fire built at the moment, but the lamp burning low showed where one had been. He had a bed arranged near one wall with her blankets and pillow, and he'd laid out the foodstuff on an outcropping that made a decent, if uneven, shelf. "You were right about this cave being perfect. You're a real lifesaver, Ellie. I mean it."

She gave him a smile and lowered the bag from her shoulder. "I brought you a hot meal—well, warm, at least. Thought we could eat together. Get caught up."

He pinned her with the same look he'd been giving her for the last twenty-eight years—ever since she was old enough to toddle after him. The look that said, "I love you, but don't push it."

Elinor sighed and crouched down to unload the food she'd brought. A tin of beans, baked for an hour in the sweet sauce Tom had loved, fresh biscuits, and roast beef. She had some chilled tea in a jar as well. "Here." She handed him one of the tin plates Tom had always taken on his hunting trips. She'd meant to send them with Franklin yesterday but had forgotten. Then added a fork. "Help yourself."

"Thanks." He filled his plate and then sat on the bedding, leaving enough room for her to do the same once she'd filled her own. He groaned over the first bite. "When did you become such a good cook?"

Elinor smiled. "Oh, about a year into marriage, I guess. I begged Tom's mother to teach me. Not that Mother didn't try before that, as you know."

They shared a laugh. Their mother was many wonderful things, but a good cook wasn't one of them.

She let him eat in peace, but once his plate was empty—hers only half so—she cleared her throat to warn him that his reprieve was over. "A marshal came by yesterday, searching for you."

Franklin went still, his gaze locking onto her face. "What did he look like? He give you his name?"

"Yes. Nathan Davis."

He lifted his brows. "And? Describe him for me."

"Tall. Really tall, probably well over six foot." She reached for the jar of tea and took a sip. Probably best not to describe him as *handsome*, though that was the word that kept popping into her mind whenever she recalled him, even if she hadn't let herself think it at the time. "Dark hair, blue eyes. Slender. He was kind. Good with Judah."

What she wouldn't say but couldn't help thinking was that if Franklin was guilty of something, Nathan Davis seemed like his best hope of fair treatment if he turned himself in.

Franklin nodded. "Anyone else come around?"

"No. Should I be on the lookout for someone?"

"No." He barked the word. "Don't look for anyone, and don't ask any questions."

Her back snapped straight. "Don't you take that tone with me, Franklin Sullivan. I'm trying to help you, remember? If you don't want that help, you shouldn't have let yourself into my kitchen."

Sighing, he squeezed his eyes shut. "I know. Sorry. I just... I don't want to drag you into all this, Ellie."

"It's a little late for that, don't you think?" Her voice still held some irritation, but she pulled the last bit of food from her bag and placed it, waxed paper and all, on his messy plate.

He unfolded the wrapping and grinned. "Chocolate cake."

"Your favorite. Now eat up and tell me what else I can do to help. And preferably, what in the world is going on."

He forked up a bite of cake and savored it before he answered. "It really is best you don't know details—for your own good, not mine. If anyone else comes around asking about me, don't say a word."

She set her plate on the stone floor. "What about the marshal?"

"Yeah." He took another bite of cake, clearly thinking it through as he chewed. "Is he still in town?"

"Should be. He said he'd be around for a few days to rest his horse and get her reshoed."

Franklin nodded. "Good. Ask him to come back to your house."

"What? Why?"

Another chunk disappeared. "Tomorrow at noon."

Unease skittered up her spine. "Answer me, Franklin. Why do you want the marshal at my house?" Because that meant he wouldn't be somewhere else? Or was her brother planning to ambush him?

Franklin met her gaze, and she felt worlds collide. The brother she knew, the one she trusted implicitly— but then this new version too, with the too-long hair, the wildness in his eyes, the weariness.

Soul-weariness or body-weariness? Here she was, able to look, and she couldn't tell the difference. Could she blame the low light, or was it her own bias blinding her? "Franklin." It was the only begging she could manage.

Her brother shook his head. "Trust me, Ellie. Please? For one more day. Just trust me."

Her hesitation probably hurt him as much as his reticence hurt her. But she nodded. "One more day."

And then what? She had no idea.

She lingered a little longer while he finished the rest of her meal. He could always sense when she'd lost her appetite. "Keep the plates and forks," she said once he was done. "Want me to wash them in the spring?"

"I'll take care of them after you go. It'll give me something to do."

"Oh, that reminds me." One more item rested in her bag, and she pulled it out and set it on his knee.

His smile was worth the extra weight it had added, and it did wonders for her heart too. Surely her brother wouldn't be so happy to see a Bible if he was guilty of murder, would he?

He ran gentle fingers over the cloth cover with its gilded cross. "Tom's?"

Her throat tightened, but she nodded. "He always kept it in the drawer of his bedside table, so he could read it before his feet even hit the floor in the morning. I left it there all this time. No one will notice its absence."

"Ellie, this means the world to me." He hugged her, giving her the chance to notice that he smelled a good deal fresher than he had yesterday. His hair and even his clothes were clean, no doubt thanks to the soap she'd sent with him. "I won't let any harm come to it, I promise. I'll return it to you. For Judah."

She kissed his cheek and then stood before the tears stinging the backs of her eyes could make good on their threat. "Judah's always in bed by eight, but I'm up until ten most nights. If you need anything, I'll leave the kitchen door open for you. Do you have a watch?"

He took out his old pocket watch, the same scratched-and-dented thing he'd been carrying since he was an adolescent. "I do. And thanks. For everything."

She prayed her smile didn't wobble. "You don't need to thank me. You're my brother."

One more hug, and then she left with her bag of empty tins, blinking her way into the daylight and blaming the sudden brightness for the continued stinging in her eyes. Following her usual routine after a solitary picnic, she went back to the house, washed her dishes, took in the laundry she'd hung out that morning, and sat with the next book she was to review for the paper, even though she had a hard time focusing on the words.

At three o'clock, she hitched up the wagon and headed into town to fetch Judah from her sister-in-law's house. She stopped at the hotel on the way, greeting the clerk as she entered. "Afternoon, Mr. Walton."

"Afternoon, Mrs. Payne. How can I help you?"

"I need to leave a message for one of your guests. The marshal, Mr. Davis."

He nodded and slid a piece of paper over to her. "I've had quite a few folks come in with messages for him. It seems this fella he's looking for has been spotted up, down, and all around Blackberry Valley."

She smiled, though she seriously doubted that. Franklin was smart enough to stay put. "I bet we're keeping the poor man hopping." She wrote her note quickly, keeping it concise.

I might have some information for you. Could you stop by my house again tomorrow? Come at noon, if you can. She debated adding that she'd be happy to provide lunch for his trouble, but that might sound too forward, given that he knew she was a widow. Rather than risk it, she simply signed her name, added a reminder about where she lived, and folded the sheet. She wrote *Mr. Davis* on the front and handed it to Mr. Walton, who slid it into a slot in the postbox behind him.

She thanked him and left. A drive to her sister-in-law's house, a quick visit, and then she and Judah were on their way home again.

The evening dragged, as did the two hours she usually relished after her energetic little boy went to bed. She jumped at every creak of the settling house and hoot of an owl, but Franklin didn't appear by ten, so she went up to bed for another restless night's sleep.

By the time dawn came, she'd once more been up for hours already, baking to work out her anxieties.

Judah certainly didn't mind the fresh muffins. She let him eat his fill and then shooed him outside, telling him she'd have lunch ready a little early. She wanted him back in before the marshal showed up, but she knew trying to keep him cooped up all morning would backfire.

Though she'd run dozens of possibilities through her mind, she had no idea what her brother had planned. Where the previous hours had dragged, the next few sped by, her stomach knotting with more dread the closer noon drew. What if Nathan Davis didn't even show up? What then?

She called Judah in for lunch at eleven thirty and stayed within sight of the window so she could see the driveway.

One worry vanished and another cinched tight when Stardust and her tall rider appeared at five till twelve, right on schedule.

She dropped a kiss onto Judah's head. "Run on up to your room for quiet time. We'll do our reading lesson after I've cleaned everything up. All right?"

Judah nodded and scurried off. Elinor waited until she heard his bedroom door close, then opened the front door and stepped outside, closing the door behind her this time. She waved a greeting to the marshal, but then all the questions she lacked answers to crashed upon her.

What did her brother mean her to do? To say? Was she supposed to keep him here for a while? And if so, how?

"Afternoon, Mrs. Payne." Mr. Davis dismounted in the same place he had the other day, but this time he looped Stardust's reins over the railing. "I trust you and your son are well?"

"Quite well, yes." Or she would be, if she didn't feel at so many loose ends. With no other guide, she'd resort to good manners. "Can I offer you a glass of iced tea?"

He gave her that soft smile she'd been thinking about more than she should have been. "I wouldn't turn it down. Gotten warm today, hasn't it?"

Had it? Come to think of it, she *was* a little warm. "Yes, it's a beautiful day." She opened the door again and ushered him inside, knowing very well that Judah would only be able to contain himself for a few minutes once he heard voices. He would try to obey her command to have his quiet time, which he knew was supposed to last until she came up to read to him. But he likely wouldn't even make it five minutes with a guest below.

She'd cross that bridge when she came to it. For now, she led Mr. Davis toward the kitchen.

And scarcely kept from shrieking when she walked into the room and saw Franklin standing there, hat in his hands and relief in his eyes. "Nathan," he said. "Thank God."

Chapter Thirteen

Hannah had known there was a spring somewhere in the cave system, thanks to Brooke, but she'd expected a nice, contained little pool. This—well, Ryan was right. It was a good thing Kayla wasn't with them. Water completely filled the floor of the chamber Hannah could barely make out in the light of Ryan's flashlight, and it also inched upward into the main chamber.

Ryan muttered something she couldn't quite catch, given that he kept his face forward, but then he turned around. "Let's hope that's not where this evidence is. I didn't bring my diving gear."

Lacy peered around them. "I'm guessing this underground stream is fed from a source to the west, where it's already raining. Water's rising fast."

She was right. In the minute or so they'd been standing there, the water had climbed higher on Hannah's boots.

Panic tried to squeeze its way into her chest. "Do you think it's safe to be in here right now?"

Ryan assessed the water. "We have a little while, at least, if we stick to the chamber on the left. It's uphill of this one."

Was it? Hannah hadn't even noticed that—but then, she'd been focusing on breathing and telling herself she wasn't *really* trapped under the earth. It was probably second nature for Ryan to take stock of things like that the moment he entered a place.

Lacy led the way back to the main chamber.

"Water on the rise in there," Ryan said to Trevor, Lexi, and Oran as they regained the larger room. "And fast. Let's head to the other chamber and see what we can find." He stepped toward the opening to the outside. "Hey, Kayla?"

"Yeah?" Her voice echoed down the crevice.

"We've got water rising in the spring chamber at a quick rate. We're going to go into the other chamber uphill from the spring, but we'll need to keep an eye on water levels."

Hannah exchanged a glance with Lacy, a bit surprised that he'd tell Kayla that now, given how nervous she would be about it. But then, they were a team, and they obviously knew that communication was crucial, especially in potentially dangerous situations. Not that this rising stream was as volatile as the waves of an incoming tide in a sea cave, but if water reached flash-flood levels, it could still trap them. Her stomach knotted at the thought.

But Ryan went on. "Want to come in and be our eyes so we can keep both cameras rolling and get all we can?"

"Yeah, let me get some of this gear off so I can fit." Kayla didn't sound anxious, at least. Just determined. And she didn't offer any of the chiding Hannah had expected.

Trevor called from the chamber on the left. "Ryan? You're going to want to get in here for sure. We've got artifacts."

"Seriously?" Ryan jogged after his camera operator.

Hannah and Lacy were hot on his trail, Oran and Lexi bringing up the rear even as Kayla's footfalls sounded in the main chamber.

Trevor had already placed lights on the edges of the oddly shaped room and had his camera trained on the entrance when they came in.

"Whoa!" Ryan said, laughing in delight as he entered. He switched off his headlamp and positioned his flashlight on a nearly level shelf in the rock wall, then turned to Hannah and Lacy. "You guys weren't kidding. There's a lot to see in here."

For the camera, Hannah grinned and nodded. For her own curiosity, she looked around to see what had them so excited. Perhaps if she focused on the waiting discoveries, she wouldn't notice how much smaller and more cramped this chamber felt.

The first things she saw were the tin plates on the shelf, glinting dully in the beams of their flashlights. They appeared old to her eyes, but she'd seen plenty of such things still around today. "How can we figure out their age?" she asked Ryan.

The show's host lifted one of the plates and turned it over in his hand. "There's a maker's mark stamped on the bottom." He held it more directly in the light. "Jackson and Sons Tinworks. Never heard of them, so we'll have to see if we can find years of operation, which could certainly help with dating it. Some makers altered their marks during different eras of their businesses, which might help us narrow it down even more. These look like they could easily be over a hundred years old, don't you think?"

When he held out a plate, Lacy took it and leaned close to Hannah so they could examine it together. They both nodded, then Lacy gave voice to Hannah's previous thoughts. "They do, but that doesn't mean they've been in here that long. We have stuff like this in the basement of my family's farmhouse too. We've used it for camping for decades."

"An excellent point," Ryan said. "As exciting as it is, these artifacts don't necessarily indicate that they were used by Franklin

Sullivan, just that they could have been." His brows creased as he pointed to something behind Trevor. "What's that though?"

Trevor backed out of the way, keeping them in the shot as they converged on the spot Ryan indicated. Hannah glanced over her shoulder and saw that Oran was fully in the chamber now too, also rolling. When she crouched down with Ryan, she had no insights to offer on the shards of broken glass. "What do you think it was?"

Ryan set several of the pieces together, jigsaw style, and said, "Aha!" when he found a circular piece. "Look at this." He pulled another piece forward. "A Bell jar, but the shape is definitely not the modern one we're used to. See this threading on the lip? It's definitely old. I'll have to look it up to be sure, but I'd say this is early 1900s."

Hannah grinned. "Our era."

"Our era," he agreed.

"Ryan, you'll want to see this," Lacy said. She'd crouched down beside them too, but rather than crowding in to look at the jar fragments, she traced something on the wall.

Hannah shone her flashlight that way, joining her beam to Lacy's. "Is that carving?"

"Absolutely," Ryan confirmed, the excitement in his voice that his viewers would be waiting for. "Are those initials? Guys, tell me if I'm wrong, but that says 'FS,' right? Doesn't it?"

Hannah's mouth went dry. The etching was faint, so she couldn't be sure part of it hadn't been eroded away by the moisture, but it sure looked like *FS* to her. "That would be my thought."

"Franklin Sullivan." Ryan repositioned slightly so Trevor could get a better shot. "I know this isn't definitive, but it builds a good case. This could absolutely be where Franklin hid out. With nothing else to do while they're hiding, people often carve their initials—even outlaws. I've seen it many times."

"What are these other marks?" Hannah pointed to a few carved etchings. "Curving line, straight line—and is that an *X*?"

Ryan's brows shot up. "*X* makes me think map. No *way*. Do you think this is a map? To where he hid the diamond, perhaps?"

Could it be? Hannah almost said she had no idea but then remembered her role. "Only one way to find out, right? We need to follow it."

Lacy leaned in. "Hard to do without scale and reference points, but let's get some good pictures and then see what we can do with Neil's maps."

Kayla poked her head into the chamber near where Lexi had stationed herself in the entrance, generally out of the way. "Just a heads-up that it's starting to rain outside, and the water's creeping into the main chamber. Maybe fifteen more minutes, then we'd better scram."

Ryan nodded. "Thanks, Kayla. All right, guys, let's check every inch of this chamber. Scour the walls, but also keep your eyes peeled for any possible hiding places."

They each moved to different parts of the cave. The chamber was about the size of Hannah's cozy living room, with a ceiling that sloped down toward the right, where it shared a rock wall with the entrance chamber. There were quite a few shelf-like rock formations and cracks that ran through them big enough for her to put a hand into, if she was brave enough.

She started with a flashlight beam instead. Who knew what creepy-crawlies waited in those holes?

The spiders she saw made her glad she'd opted for light first. Until the fourth one she flashed her beam into. The light reflected off something inside, something other than eight legs and silk webs. "Ryan? I think I've got something here."

She didn't want to say her first thought, because it couldn't be that easy, could it? That glassy chunk of near-clear something couldn't be the missing diamond, right?

Her pulse didn't care about the logic. All she knew was that she was glad she hadn't stayed outside.

Ryan moved to her side and shone his light too. "No way. No *way*!" He didn't seem to mind the old, half-dangling cobwebs like she did. He reached right in and retrieved the hunk of whatever-it-was. "Guys? Did we just find the diamond?"

Lacy squealed. "Oh my goodness!"

"I don't think that was the only thing in there, Ryan." Hannah trained her beam on the hole once more, and again light reflected back in odd ways.

Ryan passed the maybe-diamond to Lacy and reached back in. He pulled out a geode. He kept reaching in, pulling out a few other rocks, including another chunk that resembled the first one quite a bit. "Huh. Two diamonds?"

"I don't think these are diamonds." Lacy's voice had lowered to its normal register, sounding a little bummed now. "But I'm no expert, and it's hard to tell in the dark."

"Well, that would be disappointing." Ryan compared the two, holding the second one beside the one Lacy held. "Still, unless the reported size of the stolen diamond was grossly underreported and he somehow stole two, I think you may be right. These are both way bigger than thirty carats." He called, "How are we doing, Kayla?"

"Five more minutes," came her shouted reply. "And then—"

A strange noise interrupted her. A moaning sound that made the hair on the back of Hannah's neck rise. "What was that?" she whispered.

Lacy's eyes had gone round. "Um...wind?"

Ryan tilted his head, listening. A moment later, it came again. "Could be wind, I guess, but from where?"

Then the noise shifted, and Hannah could have sworn she heard it whisper, "Get out."

"Kayla? Are you hearing this?" Ryan shouted. "I don't think it's coming from in here."

"I do hear it, but I can't tell where it's coming from. It's echoing like crazy out here."

Ryan settled his gaze on Lexi, who nodded. "I'm on it." She'd had the boom mic strapped to her back, reaching out over her shoulder, but she unstrapped it as she turned and disappeared into the main chamber.

Ryan checked his watch. "We're running out of time, and there are still a lot of crevices to check. I'm going to call it. Let's get moving before the way out gets any more slippery and the water gets any higher out there. We'll come back another day. Just take note of what you're wearing, ladies, and be prepared to wear it again for continuity."

Oran handed over a canvas bag he carried, and Ryan quickly filled it with the items they'd found. "We'll take them to the house for closer examination. We'll also let Cody know what we've found, since everything is technically his. See what he wants us to do with them."

Hannah pursed her lips. If these things had belonged to Franklin Sullivan, wouldn't that make them the property of the Payne family? But then, property laws could get confusing, especially if there was language in the sale that transferred ownership of anything on the land. If something had been left somewhere for over a century, she had no idea who the rightful owner was. She was glad it wasn't up to her to untangle it.

By the time they returned to the main chamber, the strange noises had stopped and the water from the lower spring room was creeping closer to the exit. Even if they had to splash through a few inches of water to get out, Hannah knew they were fine. Still, that fact did little to keep her from craving fresh air. Especially when she saw that water streamed in through the exit as well.

"Rain has escalated to a downpour," Kayla said when they emerged. She waved toward the incoming stream. "As you can see. Let's get out of here. And step carefully on that slope out, everyone. It's really slippery now."

Oran lowered his camera. "Rain gear?"

Kayla sighed. "Yeah, I left that outside, like a genius. I'll grab it so you can get it on the equipment."

Hearing Kayla's scrambling and splashing as she climbed out did nothing to lower Hannah's unease.

"The caves must not completely fill with water," Ryan said, his voice calm and logical. "At least, not that lefthand chamber. The plates were definitely placed on that shelf purposefully, and they weren't washed away. So if that part never gets submerged, then I highly doubt the water gets very high in this main chamber."

"All the same, I vote we don't come back until it doesn't involve wading through a stream." Trevor splashed over to Lexi's side.

Lexi sent him a glance full of love and what looked like a memory of that fear leftover from the sea cave incident. "Seconded."

Kayla skidded back into the cave, handing out plastic covers for the equipment and ponchos for the people. Hannah pulled the clear plastic over her head and sent a grin toward Lacy. "This takes me back."

Lacy laughed. "Right? I haven't worn one of these since that trip to Kentucky Kingdom when we were fourteen."

Kayla turned to the opening. "Okay, let's bucket-brigade the equipment out so no one has to try to climb this hazard while carrying stuff. Hannah, Lacy, Ryan, take your places after me."

Hannah obeyed, climbing up behind Kayla and bracing her arms on the sides of the rock walls to give herself some stability. Kayla stopped at the opening and directed Hannah behind her. Hannah followed her lead and held her arms out, one toward the opening and one toward the cave, to make sure they were within arm's reach. Lacy also stopped when her hand could easily reach Hannah's.

Soon equipment appeared in Lacy's arms, and Hannah took it, then passed it on to Kayla, who set it down just outside the entrance. The cameras, the sound equipment, the boom mic, all went from hand to hand until finally Kayla signaled them to follow her outside.

Instant relief.

Rain fell in a torrent, thinning only slightly once they dashed under the cover of the trees. Hannah was more than a little surprised to see that the crew continued to film, even as they hurried through the forest and toward the Payne house.

She spent most of the trip thinking not about what they'd found at the cave, but about the coffee she would start as soon as they got to the house and the pastries that would make a good midmorning snack. Time to put aside her "local expert" role and morph back into craft services.

Everyone beelined to the mudroom entrance, Kayla going first so she could get it unlocked. They shed their wet, mud-caked boots, ponchos, hats, and jackets, and Hannah stepped into the kitchen with a happy sigh. She hadn't realized how chilly she'd been until she came into the nice, warm house.

Lacy joined her at the counter. "What are you thinking, Chef?"

"Coffee and tea, pastries, charcuterie."

"I'll put out the food if you want to take care of the coffee and hot water."

"Perfect." Hannah checked the carafes from that morning and emptied out the remnants, then poured water into the coffeepots. When she opened the cabinet in which she'd put the filters, a huff escaped her lips. "You've got to be kidding me."

"What?" Lacy moved to her side.

"The filters are missing." Normally she'd just assume Lacy had put them away somewhere else or even that she herself had tucked them into a different cabinet by mistake. But with the way things had been going, it seemed more likely that the prankster was at work again.

Lacy clearly thought the same thing, given her hum of disapproval. "I'll check bottom cabinets, you check top."

"Deal." She opened cabinet after cabinet, moved things aside, checked the boxes she'd left stacked in an unused corner, even the fridge, but nothing. Hands on hips, she glowered at the coffeepots. "I guess I can use paper towels. But this is annoying."

Lacy puffed her cheeks up with air and then let it out. "You can say that again. The roll that came with the place will probably work better. They're thinner than the ones you brought. Where'd you stash it?"

"In the pantry."

Lacy disappeared into the small room and a moment later Hannah heard her laugh. She reemerged with the filters. "They were in a box in there."

Hannah blinked at them for a moment, shook her head, and took them from Lacy. "Thanks."

The crew had dispersed into the house upon arrival but began trickling back into the kitchen as the smell of coffee lured them. Kayla, who'd gotten wetter than the rest of them, since she was caught in the rain first, had changed her clothes and now sported fluffy pink slippers that made Hannah grin. She headed, of course, to her usual stool at the counter, laptop and charger in her arms.

Lexi had added an enormous sweater to her ensemble, and she moved to the coffee station and leaned on the counter. "Perk, my darling," she crooned at the pots.

Hannah chuckled. "Sorry for the delay. The filters were hiding in the pantry."

Lexi's brows rose, then crashed. "Let me guess. Oran's ghost?"

Hannah shrugged. "Let's just say I distinctly remember putting them back in the cabinet this morning, next to the coffee."

Ryan reentered and clapped his hands, then rubbed them together. A gleeful grin stretched his mouth. "Okay, time to look at our diamonds."

"Doubtful," Lacy muttered under her breath.

Hannah chuckled.

"Pessimist," Ryan shot over his shoulder at them, his grin undaunted by the logic that was no doubt in his mind as well. He grabbed the canvas bag from the table and pulled it over to the seat he took. "Okay, Kayla. How do we identify these babies?"

Kayla typed something on her keyboard, and then her eyes moved back and forth across the screen as she read. "All right, we'll go easiest to most difficult to do at home. First, the fog test. Breathe on the stone and see how long it takes to clear. Diamonds clear quickly, other crystals more slowly."

Ryan held one of the chunks up to his mouth but paused. "This would be easier if we had something to compare it to."

Lexi abandoned her coffee vigil and moved to the table, wiggling a ring off her finger. "Here. You can test it against my engagement ring. I mean, it's not the same size, obviously, but it should give you an idea, right?"

Ryan gave her an exaggerated glance of commiseration. "Trev didn't give you a thirty-carat diamond? What a loser. I'll have a talk with him about upgrading for your anniversary."

Lexi snorted a laugh. "One carat is just fine, thanks."

Curious and having nothing else that needed her attention right this second, Hannah moved to the table in time to see the ring Lexi handed to Ryan. "Wow, that's beautiful, Lexi." The ring had a vintage-style setting encasing a gorgeous brilliant-cut diamond. "Platinum?"

"Yep. He did well, huh?"

Trevor strode back into the kitchen and smiled at his wife. "By which you mean 'he was smart enough to ask Kayla for advice.'"

Lexi rolled her eyes. "I was going to let you take the credit, you goose."

Trevor winked, then frowned. "And why are you giving your ring to Ryan? Something I should know?"

"Yeah, you totally interrupted her proposal." Ryan breathed onto the ring and stared at it, nodding. "Fog test. Okay. That really does clear off quickly. I could barely see it fog the facets at all. Let's see how these babies do." He picked up one of the rocks and breathed on it, then sighed. "That's foggy. Let's try the other."

The second behaved much like the first.

Ryan handed Lexi's ring back to her. "I'm hoping it's just the fact that the surfaces are larger. What's the next test, Kay?"

"Reflection test. Shine a light directly at them. Diamonds have colorful reflections known as fire, while other crystals don't."

Lexi set her ring on the table. "I'll just leave this here for our comparison tests."

"Grabbing a flashlight." Trevor jogged to the mudroom where they'd left most of the gear and returned a moment later with a light. He shone it first on the ring, and rainbows danced to life on the nearby wall and ceiling, sparkles shimmering within the stone too.

Hannah gave a happy sigh. "*So* beautiful. You really did well, Trevor, Kayla helping or not."

"My girl deserves the best." Trevor pulled Lexi to his side and kissed her temple. Then he turned the light on the other gems.

No rainbows, no internal fire.

Ryan folded his arms over his chest. "I'm still in denial. These aren't cut, after all. What else you got, Kay?"

"The scratch test probably won't help us. Diamonds cut glass, but so does clear quartz, and that's likely what these are. How mathematical do we feel like being? We could do a density test. Hannah, you have measuring cups and a kitchen scale with you, right?"

"Of course."

"Hey, Oran," Kayla hollered toward the door to the hallway. "We need math."

"He's our resident math nerd," Lexi explained to Hannah and Lacy. "The rest of us are amazing at screwing up basic arithmetic."

Kayla reached for a pen and paper and consulted her phone. "Okay, so the formula for density is mass over volume. Mass is weight, so Ryan, go ahead and weigh both crystals."

"You mean both diamonds." He stood.

"Diamonds count as a kind of crystal," Kayla retorted.

Hannah scurried back to the kitchen and grabbed the digital scale she'd brought with her.

"We'll indulge you for a few more minutes," Kayla told Ryan as she wrote a few words on the paper. "Oran?"

"Coming, coming." He entered the kitchen, phone in hand. "Got my calculator app up. What are we measuring?"

"Density of the crystals that probably aren't diamonds, but Ryan's in denial." Kayla drew a vertical line down the page.

"Ah, cool. Mass over volume, right?"

Ryan flashed Oran a glare. "It's so annoying that you know that without having to look it up."

Hannah turned the scale on and pressed the button to change the units from ounces to grams. Metric would give them easier numbers to work with.

Oran didn't look disturbed by Ryan's faked irritation. "My mathematical mind is what gives me great angles for *your* show."

"Yeah, yeah, smarty-pants." Ryan broke into a grin, then set the first of the rocks on the scale and read off the weight, then the other.

Kayla wrote both measurements down. "Okay, for the volume part—"

"Fill a measuring cup about halfway, record how much water is in it, add the rock, see where the water gets displaced to. The difference is the volume of the rock." Oran sent a smile to Ryan. "It's the Archimedes bathtub experiment. You know, the one that led to 'Eureka!' Or so the story goes."

Hannah retrieved her four-cup measuring cup, filled it to the metric mark halfway, and set it on the counter. "Five hundred milliliters."

Ryan lowered one of the rocks into it, careful not to splash any of the water out. He crouched down to get a straight-on view of the cup and read off the new number. Oran punched something into his phone.

"Okay, so dividing the mass by the density, we get…two point six-five-three-eight-one grams per centimeter cubed."

Ryan turned to Kayla.

Kayla sent him an "I told you so" look. "Clear quartz. Diamonds have a density of three and a half."

They repeated the process, but it gave them the same answer. Ryan sighed as he dried both crystals with a paper towel. "Well, that's disappointing."

"You know very well it's never that easy." Kayla stretched her arms above her head. "And hey, at least doing the tests gave the coffee time to finish."

"Thank goodness." Lexi rubbed her hands together.

Hannah poured the coffee into the carafes that would keep it warm without burning it. She'd no sooner gotten the lids on them than Lexi was there, opening the nozzle so it dispensed into her waiting cup.

Kayla stood, her own mug in hand. "Our next task is to come up with work we can do indoors for the next few days. Lucky for us, mysteries are more often solved in the library than out in the field."

Ryan saluted her with his empty cup. "To the library!"

Chapter Fourteen

Hannah made the crew dinner that night with Liam as her sous-chef, but when Trevor suggested they go to the Hot Spot for dessert, she certainly didn't argue. It wasn't that she didn't have plenty of dessert options for them at the house, but after only half a day stuck inside because of the rain, the adventure-seeking crew was getting stir-crazy.

Well, most of them. Kayla had been the only one who'd groaned at the idea of going out again, but she still came along rather than opting to stay back by herself.

Hannah slid into the passenger's side of Liam's Rubicon, giving him a smile. "Thanks for your help tonight."

He'd arrived later than they'd planned through no fault of his own. There'd been a five-car pileup on the interstate thanks to the rain, and he'd been out on the call. No one was seriously injured—praise the Lord—so he was in good spirits when he arrived.

"My pleasure." He gave an exaggerated bow and took her hand, raising it to his lips for a kiss. "Now. Promise me you're not going to start working as soon as we get to the Hot Spot."

She laughed. "Why would you think I'd do something like that?"

"Because I've known you for more than five minutes."

"Oh, right. That. Well, I have no intention of working." She squeezed his fingers and then reclaimed her hand so he could close her door and round the Jeep to his side. The crew had piled into the van—and she would join them on the way back to the vacation rental. She still had a bit of prep to do for breakfast in the morning but wanted to be with the crew when they were at her restaurant. When they had dinner there the other day, they drew a crowd.

Liam started the Jeep and drove slowly down the bumpy lane. "We should plan a fun date for when the show's over. Maybe catch a movie or something?"

"That sounds great." Honestly, anything with Liam sounded great, especially if it involved something other than the two of them cooking for other people. Not that they weren't having fun, but it was still *work*. And working together was different than relaxing together.

Studying his profile in the dim light of dusk, she said, "You and Ryan chatted out on the porch for quite a while after dinner. Good talk, I hope?"

He flashed her the grin that always made her heart race. "Very good. We're going to meet up for lunch on Monday. I'm working the night shift Sunday night, remember."

"I know. Dad and Uncle Gordon are going to come help with the dinner shift on Sunday and Monday, since you'll be at work." She'd tried to tell them she had it in hand, which was true, but they'd insisted. And since she figured they really wanted to come and hang out with her and the crew, she'd given up arguing and simply thanked them. "I hope you guys have fun. I knew you'd hit it off."

Liam chuckled. "He's just like he comes off on camera." He raised an eyebrow at her as he flicked his turn signal on at the end of the drive. "Right? He seems that way when I'm around."

Hannah nodded. "As far as I've ever seen. I mean, he takes it up a notch when the cameras are rolling, but it's still *him*. Just to the max, if that makes sense."

"It does. And I enjoy watching the crew together."

"Me too." He'd been right to call them a family the other night. Which made her question Lexi's theory that Oran was the one behind all the pranks. Family wouldn't treat one another like that, would they?

Then she shook her head at the thought. Family was usually the *first* to play pranks, and if they already had one prankster in their usual crew, it could make it even more likely that another would play apprentice or copycat.

At least nothing else went missing after the coffee filters.

They soon arrived at the Hot Spot. Hannah had called ahead to give Elaine a warning about the need for a table for six, and she was glad she did. The place was hopping, but her hostess led them straight to the six-top she'd held for them and brought them the dessert menu.

Hannah urged Liam to take a seat. "I'm going to see what came in today's mail and run it up to my place. Be right back."

Kayla stopped her with an outstretched arm. "Remind me where the bathrooms are?"

Hannah pointed her in the right direction and then made her way to the kitchen, greeting her staff as she went. She let herself into her office, collected the pile of mail waiting for her, and smiled when she saw a large box from an online retailer.

The gifts Marshall had sent for Raquel. Hannah carried the box up to her apartment along with the rest of the mail and grabbed a pair of scissors to open it. He'd sent a list detailing where he'd like her to hide each item around town, but pulling them out was so much more fun than just seeing them written down.

After a cursory glance to make sure nothing had been damaged in transit, she sent him a quick text letting him know she was in possession and then hurried back to the restaurant.

Kayla hadn't returned to the table yet, but Ryan stood beside the chair he'd claimed, talking to Neil. Lacy had taken his seat.

Hannah joined them with a smile, standing beside Ryan since it was closest to Lacy. "Hey, I didn't know you guys planned to come out tonight."

"Baby had a hankering for your Lava You Cake." Lacy grinned. "And Neil's indulgent. And pretty happy about it now, since it means he gets to see the crew again."

Given the number of phones out, just like the other night when they were there, Hannah suspected more people were going to "happen" by. In fact, when Neil and Lacy left with their to-go box, a somewhat-familiar woman came in, bypassing the hostess station with a wave in their direction.

Jada Jackson—she'd been the one to pass by when the crew first arrived. Hannah wasn't able to place her then, given the distraction, but now it clicked. She was the host of a lifestyle and culinary show. She'd filmed at the Blackberry Festival the previous year.

She strode their way with a flip of her hair, a smile on her face, and purpose in her step. "Ryan Hall, it's been too long."

Ryan glanced away from Liam, his smile nearly faltering. "Do we know her?" he muttered under his breath to his crew.

Lexi, Trevor, and Oran exchanged quick glances and gave miniscule shakes of their head.

"Where's Kayla?" Ryan asked, still smiling. "She's my human Rolodex."

"It's Jada Jackson," Hannah provided. "She hosts a lifestyle show on a local station."

"That does not help." But Ryan still greeted her with that smile when she reached their table. "Hello. Jada, right?"

The woman beamed. "You remember me. I *knew* we had a connection when we met at that film conference. It's been, what, ten years? Fifteen?"

Ryan laughed. "Careful, or you'll make us sound old."

Jada struck a pose—that was the only way Hannah could think to describe the pseudo-casual stance she took, one hand on the strap of her enormous designer bag, head tilted to the side. "I could hardly believe it when I heard you were in my backyard. What brings you to Blackberry Valley? We simply must get that coffee you promised me all those years ago. I can show you around."

"Ah. Not sure I'll have time." Ryan slung an arm around Hannah. "I'm mostly in town to visit my old friend."

Something flashed in Jada's eyes. Jealousy? "Really." Her gaze shifted to Hannah, who felt the need to rest a hand on Liam's shoulder for support. "I didn't realize you had Hollywood connections."

Hannah forced a smile of her own. "Well, I did live there for quite a while."

"And then she got away, and it hasn't been the same since." Ryan gave her a squeeze, effectively pulling her into his side. "And man, have I missed her."

He was clearly playing up the "old friend" bit, and Hannah suddenly remembered Kayla's claim that he'd had the two of them all but engaged when trying to ward off an overenthusiastic fan. What she didn't know was whether she was expected to play along or brush him off—neither of which felt right, especially with Liam sitting right there.

"Gracious, I leave you alone for five minutes and you replace me. I see how it is." Kayla's tone sounded playful as she approached the table, but her eyes were shrewd, calculating.

"Kayla! There's my best girl." Ryan took his arm from around Hannah and stepped to the side to pull Kayla into the space he made, twining their hands together. "And you have not been replaced. You missed Hannah too. Kay, honey, this is Jada Johnson."

"Jackson," Jada corrected, her smile downright chilly.

Kayla directed a smile to Jada that seemed to shout, "Bring it on. I can handle you," but she said, "How nice to meet you, Jada. Do you and Ry-Ry know each other?"

Hannah nearly choked on a laugh at *Ry-Ry*. Kayla had used it before, yes, but only when she poked fun at Ryan for doing something immature. Somehow, Ryan's expression didn't betray any humiliation.

Jada sized Kayla up with a long glance and apparently found her lacking. Then her gaze flicked to Hannah. "Well." She reached into her bag and pulled out a business card. She rounded the table and came up to tuck it into Ryan's shirt pocket.

The woman had guts. Hannah had to give her that.

"I'd love to catch up before you leave town, Ryan. Give me a call." She gave him a simmering smile and sashayed away.

"Rude," Kayla said. "As if his pretend girlfriend wasn't standing right here."

Ryan laughed, but he held on to Kayla's hand for another moment. That might have been for Jada's benefit, in case she looked back, but there was no way she could have seen the way he stroked his thumb over Kayla's. Frankly, Hannah wouldn't have seen it had she not been right there. "Sorry to use you as a prop before my real pretend-girlfriend came to the rescue, Hannah."

Hannah shrugged. He hadn't, in fact, said or done anything more than his usual affectionate gesture. And, more importantly, Liam seemed to find the whole situation amusing. She didn't detect any jealousy in his face or tension in his posture. Which let Hannah relax and lean against his chair. "Did you really meet her before?"

"She doesn't look familiar, and I don't usually forget a face." Ryan shrugged and pulled out Kayla's chair for her. "Still, fifteen years ago at a conference that likely had thousands in attendance and in an industry where people change their appearance like Oran changes his battery packs? It's possible, I guess."

Kayla sat. "Old 'acquaintances' started coming out of the woodwork in the last couple of years, since *Destination Discovery* got so popular."

"Most of them with a show to pitch, thinking I have an in with the network."

"Because you do," all four of his crew replied in unison, setting off a round of laughter.

Raquel approached the table, pad at the ready. "All right, guys. You decide yet?"

Ryan, stationed behind Kayla's chair like Hannah was behind Liam's, said, "Kayla just got back."

"Oh, I'll have made up my mind by the time she gets to me. Everyone else go first."

They all put in their dessert orders, except for Hannah, who was still too full from dinner. Though she halted Raquel with a hand on her arm. "Hey, do you have plans for Monday yet?" she asked in an undertone as chatter sprang up around the table.

Raquel shook her head. "Why? Need me to come in for something?"

"Oh, nothing work related. I just thought we could get together. Maybe meet for coffee?"

Raquel smiled. "Sure."

"Great. We'll figure out the time later." After Hannah had a chance to get the gifts hidden around town and had coordinated more with Marshall and Jacob on the timing for the dinner.

While Raquel moved off to put in their order, Hannah glanced around the dining room and out the wide front windows. Her perusal halted when she caught sight of someone with long legs showcased under a stylish skirt in the light from the streetlamp. Was that Jada, just standing on the street peering in at them? In the rain, no less—though she did have a polka-dot umbrella opened.

Well, that was creepy. She found herself wondering to what lengths Jada would go to get Ryan's attention. Maybe pull some pranks? Hannah couldn't see how that would play into the woman's plan, but she'd been surprised by people's behavior before.

Maybe Jada saw her looking, because she spun on her heel and stalked away. And the expression on her face in that last moment struck Hannah in a whole new way. Not attention-seeking. Jealous.

Maybe Jada really *had* met Ryan all those years ago, and maybe she'd considered them peers at the time. Maybe now she looked at the success Ryan had found and felt like she came up short. After all, her show was just a local one. It hadn't been picked up by any larger networks. Meanwhile, Ryan was touring the world and doing so well that his network kept giving him specials and spin-off shows, and he was even going to do a live comedy tour.

Maybe it wasn't about getting attention. Maybe it was about sabotage. She'd seen them arrive, after all, so she had known from the get-go they were in town.

Hannah wasn't about to cast aspersions on anyone without proof, but she'd keep her eyes open. If Jada was causing trouble, Hannah would get to the bottom of it.

Chapter Fifteen

Okay, this isn't funny anymore." Kayla stood in the center of the kitchen on Saturday morning and moved her glare over each of her crewmates. With her feet shoulder-width apart and her hands planted on her hips, she looked like a general dressing down a bunch of errant new recruits. "Where is my research laptop?"

Hannah's hand froze over the bowl of eggs she was whisking, her gaze snapping to the island they all called "Kayla's spot." Other than when they left the house and Kayla had taken to locking her laptop in her bedroom, it had been right there. But the island was void of computers.

"Why are you asking us?" Lexi, who hadn't had her first cup of coffee yet, still looked half-asleep. "We know better than to touch your gear."

"You had it in your room last night when we went for dessert." Ryan rubbed a hand over the top of his head, making his hair stand out every which way.

"Yes, and I brought it back down here to work for a while afterward." Kayla spun toward Hannah, who was flying solo at the moment. Lacy had apparently been up half the night with indigestion and was taking a nap after her morning chores before joining them. "Hannah, was it there when you came in?"

Hannah made a face. "I don't know. I didn't think to look. But I don't think so."

"Why'd you bother bringing it down here again, anyway?" Oran said around a yawn.

Kayla spun back around. "Because I don't like working where I sleep if I have a choice. And unlike in some of the places we stay, here I actually have a choice."

"Okay, but why didn't you take it back up to your room after?" Trevor didn't even look up from his phone.

"Because silly me, I thought it would be fine down here while we were all, you know, *here*." She paused, took a deep breath, and let it slowly out. "Okay, I'm going to say this once, just to get it out there. If one of you is trying to make up for Phil's absence by pulling these stunts, please stop."

Lexi glowered. "You know how I feel about pranks. They're juvenile, stupid, counterproductive, stupid, annoying, and—"

"Stupid." Trevor glanced up, smiling. "And I wouldn't dare, given my wife's opinions, because I'd be sleeping on the couch for participating in something so juvenile, counterproductive, and—"

"Stupid." Lexi reached over and patted his hand. "Thank you. I love you too."

Ryan sighed and looked at Oran, just as Kayla, Trevor, and Lexi did too.

Oran's eyes went wide. "What? You can't think it's *me*? How long have you known me? And when have I ever done something like this?"

"You and Phil have gotten awful tight," Kayla said.

"And some of us," Ryan said with a glance at Kayla, then Lexi, "have been a little hard on you lately about the ghost stuff."

"And you're the one who supposedly noticed the missing van key. You could have just faked the whole thing, had it in your pocket." Lexi sounded almost, but not quite, apologetic as she pointed it out. "Anyone could have moved the other stuff, but you're the only one who doesn't drink coffee. Only someone who doesn't drink coffee would be so cruel as to mess with the filters."

Oran pushed back from the table. Hannah had never actually seen him angry, but he was clearly not only upset but hurt. "I've poured blood, sweat, tears, and years of my life into this show. Into *all* your shows," he said to Ryan. "If you really think I would do anything to hurt or even inconvenience one of you, you clearly don't know me at all." Abandoning his cup of tea, he stormed down the hall.

"Oran," Kayla called after him, "we're sorry. We don't think—where are you going?" From her vantage point, Kayla must have been able to see way more than Hannah could.

"Out. Away from all of you for a few blessed minutes." Seconds later, the front door slammed.

Hannah winced, flipped on the heat underneath the skillet she had ready, and went back to whisking the eggs.

Lexi sighed. "He didn't deny it."

"Lex, drop it. It's not Oran," Ryan said, sounding rather irritated himself.

The coffeepots had finished dripping, so Hannah poured them into the carafes. Perhaps a jolt of caffeine would serve to chase away some of the grumpiness in the room.

The front door opened and closed again, making everyone pause and look toward the doorway. Oran came through it a minute later, still obviously upset, but with a laptop in hand. He shoved it at Kayla. "It was in the van."

Kayla took it with a frown. "I didn't put it there—and I'm not saying you did either, Oran. Okay? I'm sorry. Really."

Oran just grunted, pivoted, and left again.

After holding her hand a few inches above the skillet to test the heat, Hannah added a dollop of butter, tilted the pan so the butter skated everywhere to coat the surface, and then poured in the eggs.

"I hate to mention it," Kayla mumbled, "but the power supply is still missing."

Everybody spread out to search the house. Hannah couldn't exactly abandon the eggs, so she kept her focus where it belonged... though she did check in the fridge for any oddly placed power supplies when she retrieved the shredded cheese, cubed ham, and salsa for the scramble. Nothing but food met her gaze.

She had eggs piled on a platter and buttered toast cut into triangles by the time everyone returned, empty-handed, to the kitchen. The sound of a car door slamming made her glance out the window toward the driveway.

If Oran had left, he hadn't gone far, because he was striding from the van past the Jeep when he stopped, glanced through the window, and with wide eyes, opened the door and pulled out the missing power cord. "Looks like Oran just found it," Hannah said over her shoulder. "In the Jeep. He saw it as he walked by."

"Not suspicious at all," Lexi muttered.

"Lex, enough. I'm serious." Ryan's steps sounded, heading from the kitchen to the front door, which soon opened. "The hero! Dude, if you hadn't gotten mad and stormed out, I don't know how long we would have been looking before someone thought to check the vehicles. Sorry you were upset, but seriously, I'm glad you went out there."

Oran said nothing, at least nothing Hannah could hear, but he returned with Ryan and took his seat again, his rain jacket presumably left on the coat tree by the front door along with his shoes.

Hannah carried the platters to the table and paused to rest a hand on Oran's shoulder in silent encouragement.

He sent her a close-lipped smile in response.

"Anyone want juice?" she asked. A couple of people raised their hands, so she brought out the juice and some glasses, then went back for the potato casserole finishing in the oven.

Kayla had been busy plugging in and powering up her laptop. Now she frowned at something on the screen. "Um, guys? I shut this down last night like I always do when I'm done for the day, but just now it was only asleep, and it came back up with a browser page open, along with a document."

Ryan paused in pulling out his chair. "Do we want to know?"

Hannah slid the baking dish of potatoes onto a trivet she'd placed on the table. She tugged the oven mitts off her hands and paused behind Kayla.

The document displayed a few words in giant type. *Let me rest in peace.* Hannah frowned as Kayla read it out loud, adding, "And then the browser has one tab open. It's an archived article from the Lexington newspaper. It's dated April 1910 and details how Franklin

Sullivan, murderer and diamond thief, was killed on a farm outside Blackberry Valley."

Hannah glanced at the table to see everyone's reactions. Oran's eyes had gone wide, Trevor scowled, and Ryan pointed at Lexi. "Don't say a word," he said.

Lexi, looking a bit more like her usual self now that she'd had some coffee, raised her hands in surrender.

"Can *I* say a word?" Oran tapped his finger on the table. "Ghost."

Kayla sighed. "Oran, a person wrote this, not a ghost. Even assuming for a moment that they could exist, how would a dead guy from 1910 know how to operate a computer? And if they pass through walls, how would he be able to type?"

Oran lifted his nose in the air. "You think those still moving among us haven't picked up a few things?"

Kayla turned her face away from Oran and toward Hannah. She moved her mouth, though no sounds came out. She was counting, like Ryan had done the other day with Brooke.

Hannah turned away to hide her grin. Maybe they'd taken the same course on keeping one's temper with colleagues.

"Okay, enough. Let's say grace and eat, okay?" Ryan sat, and Kayla followed, motioning Hannah to take what had become her usual seat beside her.

It still felt a little strange to be eating with the people she was hired to serve, but in a nice way. She joined hands with Kayla and Lexi, silently praying that Lacy got the rest she needed.

After Kayla prayed aloud, Ryan scooped eggs onto his plate and said, "Okay, lay out our day for us, Kayla. Caving is clearly out, but what else have you come up with?"

"Everyone's favorite thing," Kayla announced with a mischievous smile. "Research. Some can be done online here, like looking up the maker of those tin plates, for starters. But I have a list of things for us to check on in town too. I've talked to the head of the historical society—thank you for that info, Hannah—and we set up a meeting at the library for ten o'clock this morning." Kayla added a triangle of toast to her plate and reached for the potatoes.

"That doesn't sound like enough to keep everyone busy," Trevor pointed out.

"Oh, but it does. The library changed its hours for us—they're usually open nine to three on Saturdays, but today they're doing eleven to five so we have full run of the place this morning. We want to honor the trouble they went to for us, which means two hours to film in there and not a minute more. We'll need everyone for that portion."

Ryan poured himself a glass of orange juice. "Do we know if the library has anything worth filming?"

"They have records of Elinor Sullivan marrying Thomas Payne, including photographs of the wedding that include Franklin Sullivan," Kayla replied.

"Good enough for me." Ryan took a sip of his juice. "And Neil Minyard said he'd close the shop for a while if we wanted to do a segment in there, with his maps. I told him about the carving on the wall and said we'd forward some images of that for him to try to match up with his references. We could do that this afternoon, or tomorrow or Monday. Whatever's best for him and you, Kayla."

"We could reach out to Ford again too," Oran said around a bite of toast. "See if he's dug up old family photos or something."

"And we should have filmed the testing of the crystals. We could redo that this afternoon or tomorrow even." Trevor scooped a heaping spoonful of potatoes onto his plate. He looked at Ryan, Kayla, then Hannah. "I'm guessing that, as usual, you're taking tomorrow morning off for church?"

Kayla nodded. "Figured we'd tag along with you, if that's okay, Hannah."

She smiled. "Perfect. Just like old times."

Kayla got back to business. "As for the rest, I already sent a text to Ford, and I have filming the tests on the crystals down for this afternoon. It would be a fun little science bit. We don't get to do those often—though, Oran, you'll have to coach Ry on the math so it looks like he's doing it." At Oran's snort of laughter and Ryan's feigned indignation, Kayla grinned and then glanced around the kitchen. "We'll have to set up the lights for that, given the lack of natural light while this storm's hovering over us, but I'm thinking the kitchen makes the most sense for it—assuming we won't be too much in your way, Hannah."

"I'll work around you guys. No worries at all."

"Great. If you want to pass me Neil's info, Ryan, I'll loop him in and see what works best, but I'm thinking Monday for the map segment. His website says he's closed tomorrow and Monday, and I don't want to horn in on family time after church."

Ryan nodded. "Monday works for me. Looks like we might get a break in the weather tomorrow afternoon anyway, so let's do some more drone shots and see if the cave's passable again yet."

Lexi scooped eggs onto her toast but paused with it halfway to her mouth, eyes on Hannah. "Don't suppose to you want to be a grip today?"

Hannah's brows went up. "A what?"

"Grip." Lexi grinned. "It's what we call someone whose job is... well, to grip something. In this case, the boom mic for me. I'll position you. It's way easier with two people on sound."

"Oh. Sure." It was surely more complicated than Lexi made it out to be, but she'd take the excuse to tag along and see what Phyllis Taft, head of the historical society, had found for them.

"Am I the only one still stuck on the laptop mysteriously ending up in the van?" Ryan set his fork down and leveled his gaze on Kayla. "Maybe we should call the cops. Have them dust for prints."

"And get that powder on my computer? Um, no." Kayla stabbed a potato.

"Ghost don't have fingerprints," Oran muttered into his food.

Kayla ignored him. "Besides, it's obviously someone who can get in and out of the house, which narrows it down. Let's just talk to Ford and see who might have a key, or the code from a previous stay or something."

"Not a code—the app." Ryan frowned and leaned on his elbow. "But Brooke might have a key. She was clearly not happy that we went ahead without her, and she knows her way around the place."

Hannah swallowed her bite of toast. "Her dad wasn't happy she was out here. And from the sound of it, he got her a job that she put at risk by taking a day off. Worth asking how deep their tension runs, I guess. I can't think he'd risk doing anything that would get a bad review or worse on his rental property, but it's possible Brooke could want to sabotage him, not just you guys, if she's angry with him."

Kayla considered that with a rock of her head back and forth. "She's a little old to still be in her rebellious years, but there was definitely tension there. I wonder if we could get access to the doorbell camera? That would show us who's coming and going."

Ryan snapped his fingers and pointed at Kayla. "Gold star. Why didn't we think of that before? For that matter, we could put some other cameras around the house to catch the culprit."

"We could." Her tone, accompanied by the furtive glance around the table, said she didn't think it would do much good if it was one of their own. "Not sure if we can blame the weird noises in the cave on her though. Lexi, did you have any luck analyzing it?"

"Some. Nothing that really answers our questions, but it definitely sounded different from the voices of everyone else in the cave. It didn't echo in quite the same ways, which could be because of where it originated, or because of something else." Lexi shrugged. "Cave acoustics are weird. But the craziest part was this little blip I could see in the wave form. When I isolated that and cranked it up, it sounded like a dog barking."

They all stared at her for a long moment. Hannah glanced at Kayla and Ryan, but they didn't seem to have any ideas. "I didn't see or hear a dog anywhere near the cave." Kayla said. "Anyone else?"

They all shook their heads.

"Not to say the mic couldn't have picked up something our ears didn't," Lexi said. "It happens a lot. But I haven't heard any dogs around here either."

They tossed a few other theories around as they finished eating. Kayla finished first, so she grabbed her phone to text Ford about the doorbell camera. Hannah hurried to get the cleanup done before they had to leave for the library. She was putting the leftovers into the fridge when Kayla said, "Ford says he'll review the footage and send us anything that could be helpful, but all he's seen when he gets alerts is us coming and going. And that one blur we're calling a moth."

"Well…" Ryan's voice was quiet, serious. Hannah turned from the fridge and found that only he and Kayla were still in the kitchen. "If it's one of us doing this stuff, that would make sense."

Kayla frowned. "I really don't think it's Oran." Her voice matched his in both volume and intensity.

"I don't either. But Lexi's been frustrated with him lately. What if she's doing it to frame him?"

Kayla winced. "How awful."

"I know. I don't like the idea either, and I can't quite square it. But come on—who else is going to take her toothbrush?"

Hannah couldn't shake the feeling that this division in the crew was far worse than any missing items. "Can I butt in with some unsolicited advice?"

Kayla smiled at her. "Always."

"Don't blame each other, whatever you do. What you have with this crew—it's special. Take it from someone who's worked with a lot of teams in a lot of kitchens, some great and some horrific." She looked from Kayla's face to Ryan's and back again. "It's rare to find what you guys have. Some frustration is natural, like with any family, but don't let it make you turn on each other. Not with only vague suspicions to go on."

"You're right." Kayla let out a long breath and bumped her shoulder into Ryan's. "I mean, unless we're turning on Ry. That's allowed."

"Don't start something you can't finish, Kay." Impish grin in place, he bumped her in return, hard enough to send her back a step. He caught her, and they both laughed.

Hoping that talking to the two leaders of the team would ensure that the message trickled down to the others, Hannah turned back to her cleanup. She finished the dishes just as Kayla called out that it was time to go and everyone should lock up their stuff.

Since the trip to the library was officially part of the show, Ryan drove the Jeep, complete with cameras set up to record him and whatever funny or insightful things he might say on the way. And of course, that meant making the trip from the house to the main road multiple times so Trevor and Oran, they and their cameras all in rain gear, could get a few shots of him driving through the puddles. Oran even got out the drone to capture it, since the rain was light enough.

Hannah stood outside as they filmed. Realizing this was the first time she'd really lingered at the front entrance—she usually went straight to the kitchen door—she took a moment to admire the fossils in the rocks on the path. She crouched down for a better view.

Footprints where grass gave way to mud around the path caught her eye, and she followed a few imprints from the path to the side of the house, toward the kitchen. They weren't necessarily out of place, given how often the crew used the kitchen entrance too. But something about them bothered her. What was it?

She leaned closer. The prints weren't huge, but they were big enough to rule out most of the women—Kayla, Lexi, Hannah, and Lacy all had feet much smaller than this. They'd chatted shoes over lunch the other day, when Lexi had complained that her boots were wearing out and she needed a new pair.

That was what was wrong. Every single member of the crew wore boots, but these prints lacked that kind of tread pattern. They were smooth, smoother even than an athletic shoe. They looked more like they were made by a dress shoe. A man's? Or a woman with larger feet? Jada was tall enough to have feet this size, and she certainly didn't wear boots. Well, not ones with tread. On the other hand, any dress shoe she wore would more than likely have heels, which would leave a much different print than these.

"Okay, all done," Oran called out as he caught the drone.

Kayla clapped. "Great. Everyone saddle up."

Oran no sooner got the drone put away than the heavens unleashed their torrents again. Hannah put up her rain jacket hood and rushed into the van with the others, where she could ask Lexi for tips on being the grip for the boom mic as they headed into town for real.

Lexi grinned at her. "You hold it steady and point it where I tell you. That's it."

Kayla laughed. "You also have to keep it out of the camera shot, but as close as possible to that line, so we pick up the best audio we can."

"As I said. Steady and where I tell you. Easy-peasy." Lexi winked and positioned her headphones over her ears. "You'll be great. Don't worry about it."

They soon arrived at the library, where head librarian Evangeline Cooke held the door open as the crew bustled their equipment indoors.

"Thanks for rearranging your schedule for us, Evangeline," Hannah said as she slipped inside, miscellaneous bags full of who-knew-what on her shoulders.

Evangeline smiled. "Happy to help. Phyllis is already waiting with the historical society stuff."

Hannah looked over her shoulder to see who else was coming and paused when another car parked in the lot. Mrs. Bryant got out, eyes on the crew.

Phyllis waved. "Sorry, ma'am! Library has special hours today for an event. It's not open to the public for a couple of hours yet."

Hannah's old science teacher met her gaze for a moment, then bit her lip. "I was hoping to speak with Ryan Hall. I saw the crew heading this way from the old Payne place."

As in, she'd followed them?

Kayla, arms now empty, stepped outside. "Hello. I'm Kayla Dreher, research director for the show. I'm afraid Ryan's busy, but can I help you with anything?" Kayla was doing what she did best—protecting Ryan's time.

Mrs. Bryant sighed but renewed her smile. "I found some documents I thought might be useful for your investigation, but I only have about half an hour before I have to be somewhere. I was hoping to catch you all first."

Kayla checked her watch and pursed her lips. "I'm so sorry. We really have to get moving on this so we don't inconvenience the library any longer than necessary. Could we set up another time?"

Mrs. Bryant's shoulders sagged a little. "Sure. I can come back another day."

Kayla hustled over to pass the older woman a business card. Figuring everything was under control, Hannah went inside. Kayla followed a few seconds later.

While the crew got set up, Hannah drifted over to where Phyllis and Kayla chatted. Phyllis greeted her with a smile and motioned to the boxes she had sitting on a table. "Feel free to take a look. I got through what I could yesterday and this morning, but the Paynes have been in Blackberry Valley from the start, so they're mentioned in a lot of things—or could be, anyway. I've pulled the photographs and articles from the newspaper archives and printed them out, but there's still plenty to go through."

"Can we see the photo you found that has Franklin in it?" Kayla asked. "I'd love to put a face to the name."

"Of course." Phyllis opened a manila folder sitting beside the boxes and handed her an enlarged photo printed on glossy paper.

Hannah studied it with Kayla. It was clearly old and a bit grainy, probably thanks to being enlarged, but she had no trouble making out the wedding party. The bride, Elinor, stood in a Gilded Age white dress, a beautiful lace veil over her hair and a bouquet in hand that trailed flowers all the way to the ground. Her groom gazed down at her with pure adoration on his face. A line of women stood at her side, men on the groom's. Which was Franklin?

Phyllis picked up a notecard. "This was the caption on the photo, which named everyone from left to right. Franklin Sullivan is the man on the end."

As soon as she said it, Hannah could see the resemblance between him and the bride. He was a handsome man, probably in his midtwenties in the photograph, and looked pleasant. Kind. Something about the way his eyes crinkled as he smiled gave her the impression of someone who found joy in life—though maybe she was reading too much into it.

"And this was what year?" Kayla asked.

"Let's see." Phyllis checked the printed article. "This says 1902."

"Eight years before his death." Hannah sighed. "A lot can happen in eight years. He didn't live around here, though, did he?"

"I don't think so," Phyllis said. "The article about the wedding called him a 'decorated police officer from Chicago, Illinois.' And I haven't seen his name anywhere else in my browsing. Well, aside from the articles in the Lexington paper about him being on the run from the law and then being shot and killed."

Hannah frowned. "The Lexington paper. Not a local one?"

Phyllis shook her head. "No, nothing about him was in the local paper. I did find that odd, given that his sister lived here at the time. But there's absolutely no mention of him in our paper, nor of his connection to Elinor Sullivan Payne in the Lexington paper."

"I don't know what to make of that." Hannah reached into the nearest box and pulled out a collection of documents yellowed with age.

Kayla tilted her head, eyes distant in thought. "A low-key cover-up, maybe? Was Elinor Payne an important figure in the community?"

"Not as far as I can tell." Phyllis shrugged. "I found a record of her selling off most of the farmland attached to the Payne property after her husband Thomas passed away. But she kept the house and surrounding acres. Those were passed on to her son, Judah. I couldn't find any mention of her after 1911. The only Payne I spotted after that was Judah—he was active in the local school, then went off to college and eventually became a professor at UK in Lexington. He kept a house there but also here, spending summers and weekends on his family homestead and pouring his love for geology into it."

Phyllis fished another stack of photos from her folder. "These were featured in a 1963 article about the way he incorporated geology into his house."

Hannah smiled at the images Phyllis flipped through. "Yeah, the house still looks like that—I mean, the structure and all the geology. The furniture and accent pieces have been updated."

"So what happened to Elinor?" Kayla flipped through another stack of documents from the box. "If Judah grew up here, she must have still been in the area too, right?"

Phyllis shrugged. "Not sure. I didn't see her mentioned in these articles. Could mean nothing, or it could be she died when he was a child. Keep in mind this was about half a decade before the Spanish Flu pandemic. It's hard to say. I'm sure there are clues somewhere in all this, but I haven't had time to really dig through it."

Hannah exchanged a glance with Kayla. "Well, the crew's going to have a few more rain days when they'll be stuck inside. Could we borrow this stuff and bring it back to you next week?"

"I don't see a problem with that," Phyllis said.

"Great." Kayla glanced up when Ryan waved an arm. "And it looks like we're set up. Let me get you a release form and a mic, Phyllis, and then we'll get started."

Chapter Sixteen

The Payne Farm

April 14, 1910

Elinor could only stare as Nathan Davis surged forward and—in a move she never would have expected—enveloped her brother in a fierce hug.

"Frank, praise the Lord. I thought I'd never catch up with you." The marshal pulled away, and Elinor edged toward a chair so she could sink onto it. He glanced her way, brows furrowed. "Pardon me, ma'am. You must be wondering what a stranger is doing in your kitchen."

Franklin laughed. "Nate, this is Ellie. My sister."

She could see realization dawn in his eyes. "This is Ellie. You never actually mentioned her full name, nor her married one, and she introduced herself as Elinor Payne. I didn't make the connection. And the boy is Judah?"

Her brother quirked a brow her way. "You said he was kind to Judah. I assumed that meant they'd been introduced. I thought you came here because you knew who they were, Nate."

Mr. Davis shook his head. "No, I just talked to everyone I could around here when I saw the sign you'd left for me, pointing me this way. Figured you were avoiding large areas of population and came through here where you wouldn't be recognized. When I met the boy I said something about him being the man of the house. He played along and said he was Mr. Payne. I never learned his given name."

Franklin pulled out a chair at the table and motioned for Mr. Davis to do the same. "When Ellie said a marshal had asked about me and gave me your name, I wasn't sure I could believe it. You know Randolph impersonated you back in Memphis. I figured I needed to get you here where I could verify your identity."

"Randolph?" Elinor squeezed her eyes shut for a moment, rubbing at her temples. "Could someone please tell me what's going on?"

"Sorry." Franklin reached over and rested his hand on her wrist. "I left the Chicago police force two years ago."

"And joined the US Marshals," Davis added before she could panic. "We brought him on specifically to go undercover with the Irish Mafia and anarchists in Chicago, so he couldn't tell anyone about his new job, not even his family."

Relief left her boneless. Not an outlaw, but a lawman, still. Her gaze flew back to her brother. "But that
means you have been working with those criminals.
Not as a criminal yourself, but that makes it even more
dangerous, doesn't it? If you're found out?"

Franklin's expression grew sober. "It's a risk I
had to take, Ellie. These groups are growing more
and more powerful in Chicago and finding sup-
porters from all over the country to bankroll them,
often through operations that are both illegal and
unsavory." His eyes gleamed with that familiar
passion.

How had she doubted him for even a minute?
She knew her brother. She turned her wrist over so she
could clasp his hand. "So what's this business about
the diamond?"

Franklin flicked his gaze to Mr. Davis, who sighed.
"We had a tip that Carl Parson, the son of one of the
anarchists executed in 1887 after the Haymarket Riot,
had somehow come into possession of a thirty-carat
diamond, which he intended to sell to finance the
group his father had died for."

"I'd already convinced Carl I was sympathetic
to his cause," Franklin interjected. "So I was sent to
Arkansas to intercept him before he could make
the sale to an industrialist in St. Louis. I managed
to catch up with him around Jonesboro." This he
directed toward Mr. Davis. "But he didn't buy that

the anarchists had sent me to help. He thought I was trying to steal the diamond for myself."

The marshal frowned. "He didn't suspect you were a lawman, though, did he?"

Franklin shook his head. "No. But he came at me with a gun and took a shot at me. I fired back in self-defense. He didn't make it."

Not murder, but a man had ended up dead. Elinor gave his fingers another squeeze. She knew how that would weigh on her brother. Franklin had always believed that every life was sacred, beloved of the Lord. He had always worked to preserve life, not to take it.

Clearly Nathan Davis knew this about him too. "I'm sorry," he murmured. "I know that's not how you wanted it to go down. What about the diamond? You recovered it?"

Franklin nodded. "I have it stashed somewhere safe."

She expected the marshal to demand he hand it over immediately. Instead, Mr. Davis said, "Good. Keep it wherever you have it for now. I'm pretty sure the other Parson brothers were following me."

What did he mean by following him? Had they followed him here? Were they in danger?

"What?" Franklin snapped to attention. "I knew they were heading to St. Louis to meet up with Carl, but I haven't detected them on my tail yet."

Mr. Davis waved toward the window. "I saw them when I approached town a couple of days ago. They didn't come *into* town, so I figured I'd stick to my pattern. They'll keep following me when I leave again, I'm sure. Probably think that's the easiest way to get to you. So I'll lead them away from the path you take, but it's best if I don't have the diamond."

His expression said it all—that he expected to be attacked at some point. Why else would it be best? "And you just accept that?" Elinor blurted before she could stop herself. "That violent criminals will keep following you to get at my brother? That they could try to kill you?"

"It's the risk we take for the job." He didn't sound merely accepting, but rather completely resigned. Almost defeated.

She glanced at Franklin, but he shook his head. And before she could think of something else to say, little footsteps raced their way. Judah flew into the kitchen, face alight. "Uncle Franklin! I thought it was your voice!"

Elinor loved watching her brother with her son. All traces of the stern lawman disappeared, melting into the fun-loving, caring boy she'd always counted on to be her rock. He held his arms open, and Judah rushed into them. Franklin scooped up the child and settled him on his lap.

Judah chattered happily. "I got the geodes you sent me last month. And I've found so many fossils. I'll show them to you before you go. How long are you staying? I can take you out for a rock hunt, like we did last summer. I bet we'll find lots. I always find more when you're here. Did you find anything fun in Chicago?" Then he turned to Mr. Davis. "You can come too, if you want. Uncle Franklin's the best at rock hunting."

Mr. Davis's lips tugged up, the resignation fading away. "Is he now?"

Judah nodded. "He's sent me so many rocks." His head swung back toward his uncle. "Did you bring me any new ones this time?"

"Judah." Her son knew not to beg gifts from people, generally speaking, but she'd never been quite sure if rocks fit in that category. And her brother did always have something interesting in his pocket for her little boy.

He ducked his head. "Sorry, Mama."

But Franklin grinned. "You didn't think I'd come see you without any, did you? Nate, would you get my bag? It's by the back door."

The marshal obliged and set the bag on the table.

"Okay, let's see what we've got here." Franklin opened the bag and pulled out a rock that seemed nondescript from where she sat. "I've been traveling a good bit, so I've picked up things from all over for you."

Tears stung her eyes. Her brother had been fleeing from criminals after killing a man in self-defense, and he'd still taken the time to collect geology samples for her son?

Judah exclaimed over each piece, the ones that looked like normal rocks as well as the crystals and geodes in various colors, the fossils, the amber.

Mr. Davis caught her eye and tipped his head toward the porch. "Have a minute?" he asked softly.

Knowing her brother and son wouldn't even miss her, she nodded and led the way out onto the porch. The marshal followed, moving to the far end, where Tom's cousin had just hung up the swing again for her after its winter in the barn.

She didn't sit though. "Tell me the truth," she said, keeping her voice to a whisper. "How dangerous are these men following you two?"

His expression was so telling that he didn't have to answer, but he must have chosen to anyway. "I won't lie to you. They're extremely dangerous. The only thing they have any loyalty to is their own family, so if they know Frank killed Carl—which they surely do, given that the papers somehow got wind of it—they won't rest until he's dead."

She wrapped her arms around her middle, even though she knew she wouldn't find an anchor in herself. It was the Lord she clung to, begging Him to help even as she searched for words to say to this man before her. "What can I do to help?"

He shook his head firmly. "Nothing. You've already put yourself and your son at too much risk by helping him. I know you had to, that he's your brother. And I know he wouldn't have come here in the first place if he wasn't sure he could insulate you from the risk. With any luck, the Parsons are as ignorant about who you are to him as I was. But all the same, if you have family you could take Judah to visit, preferably on your late husband's side, now would be a fine time to put some distance between you and your brother."

Her first instinct was to refuse, but she held her tongue. She'd have to consider the wisdom of his recommendation. Not for her own sake, but for Judah's. "I'll give it some thought."

"Good." He started back toward the door.

"Mr. Davis—"

"Please. It's Nathan." He faced her again, that soft smile on his lips. "I realize you don't know me from Adam, but Frank has told me all about you and Judah to the point I feel as if I know you. Well, aside from the rather pertinent details about your actual name."

It made her smile, to think of her brother telling his friend about her and Judah. And warmed her insides in an unexpected way to consider that this fellow had been thinking of her as *Ellie*, something only Franklin had ever called her. "All right," she said, still softly. "Nathan. And you can call me Elinor—or Ellie. Either's fine."

Heavens, but now was not the time to turn to mush at a handsome man's gaze, his grin. "Thank you. He speaks of you often, you know. How proud he is of you, carrying on after Tom's death as you've done. How you're raising an amazing little boy. I don't have any family left, so...well, I guess I've been living on his stories since we met three years ago."

"Three?" Her brows lifted. "I thought he said two."

"Two since he joined us. But we met and became friends a year before that. It's how I knew we could trust him for the job." His face went serious again. "And I guess that means the blame is mine for his current situation. I'm the one who recruited him to be a marshal."

He said it like she'd hold it against him. And true, she didn't like the danger of the situation. But she knew her brother. "He's always dreamed of becoming a federal agent of some kind. I imagine he views it not as blame, but as credit."

"I see you're every bit as kind and generous as he's made you out to be." Nathan passed a hand through his dark hair. "Thank you for that."

Amusement caught hold of her. "It's no odd thing, you know. To be kind."

"Isn't it?" He shook his head, his blue eyes going stormy. "Feels like it sometimes, in my line of work. Not sure how much longer I have it in me, to be honest.

I've been considering, after this case—well. I won't bore you with my life story."

"You could." The words slipped out before she could stop them. "I wouldn't mind."

For someone who said kindness was in short supply, he certainly exuded it, especially when he smiled. "Perhaps I'll take you up on that sometime." He turned toward the fields. "This is a nice area. Don't tell Frank I said so, but it beats Chicago any day of the week."

She laughed. Her brother was definitely a city boy, and she'd once thought herself a city girl too. But it hadn't taken long to realize she preferred the quiet of the countryside. That was one of the many reasons she hadn't moved back to Chicago after Tom's death. "I agree with you there. This place, these people, made me feel like one of them, even though I'm a Yankee. It's a good place to make a home, have a family. And I can't imagine Judah, with his love of nature, thriving in a city. I'm never even sure where Franklin finds the things he sends him."

"Shops." Nathan chuckled. "He's learned to watch for interesting things whenever he's out of the city too, but mostly he buys them."

Franklin had never told her that. "Well, that feels like cheating."

He winked and turned her to mush again. "Don't tell him I told you. Wouldn't want to tarnish him in his nephew's eyes."

"I won't breathe a word." Having no other excuse to linger out here with him, she didn't halt him this time when he headed toward the door.

She wasn't surprised to find that Judah's full rock collection—all five boxes of it—had appeared on the kitchen table. He and Franklin were bent over it, turning something or other over in their hands, heads together. The new pieces her brother had brought must have already been sorted, categorized, and put in their new homes.

Judah looked up at her, no shadow in *his* eyes to mar the day. "Mama, can Uncle Franklin and I go rock hunting by the stream? Can we?"

Panic flared in her brother's eyes to match the flame of it in her chest. "I wish I could," her brother said before she could object, "but not today. I was only stopping in for a minute."

Judah frowned. "You always stay for at least a week."

"I know, buddy. But I just detoured to say hello on my way home. Business trip."

Judah frowned but didn't ask what kind of business. His lower lip began to tremble.

"Aw, Jude. Listen." Franklin put a knuckle under Judah's chin. "I'll come back soon, okay? I promise. I know short visits are hard, and I wish I could stay longer too. But I'm awful glad I got to see you. A little time's better than none at all, right?"

Judah sniffled and rubbed his nose, but nodded.

Franklin gathered him into a tight hug and kissed the top of his head. "Tell you what, kiddo. I'll come visit again for your birthday. All right? I'll stay *two* weeks then."

Did that mean that he expected this case or mission or whatever it might be called to be over and done with by June? She hoped so.

"Promise?" Judah clung to him.

"Promise."

Judah pulled back and turned to look up at the marshal. "How come you didn't mention the other day that you're my uncle's friend?"

Nathan put his hands on his hips. "How come *you* didn't mention you're my friend's nephew?"

Judah giggled. "I didn't know you knew him!"

"And I didn't know *you* knew him. But now we both know, so let's start over." He held out his hand, much like he had before. "I'm Nate, your uncle Franklin's friend."

Judah shook his hand, grinning from ear to ear. "I'm Judah. Your friend Franklin's nephew."

"Nice to meet you, Judah. Your uncle's told me all about you, and it's an honor to make your acquaintance."

Franklin, meanwhile, had stood and was looking toward the door. "I better not linger long. And before you ask, Ellie, I don't need anything else. You've got me well stocked, and I'll be heading out as soon as it's dusk."

Elinor wanted to stop him but knew she couldn't. So she settled for giving him a long hug. "Send me a wire when you can. Let me know you got home safe."

"I will. And Ellie, thanks. For everything."

"I already told you. You don't have to thank me. I wish you'd let me do more." She squeezed him as hard as she could. "Love you."

"Love you too." He kissed her temple and drew away, kneeling to get another hug from Judah.

Nathan reached for the hat he'd left on the table. "I'll head out too and go back to town." His gaze moved to Elinor. "But I'll stop by once more before I head to... Nashville, Franklin?"

Franklin considered for a moment and nodded. "That'll do."

"Good." He put his hat on, tipping it to her in the process. "It's good to meet you properly, Elinor. And you, Judah."

Elinor set her hands on her son's shoulders. "We'll see you out, Nathan." Much as she wanted to see her brother to safety, if someone *was* watching from up by the road, it would look odd if she didn't walk the marshal to the door.

A few more words of farewell between the men, and they turned toward their separate doors. Elinor nudged Judah along with her to the front, but she made no objection when he wiggled away and went back inside rather than come out with her. She could tell he was scarcely holding in his emotions and respected that he didn't want to cry in front of the marshal.

Nathan sighed. "Let's pray the Parson brothers follow me to Nashville. I'm not sure if they followed Franklin or me this far, but I'm glad I got to talk to Franklin for a few minutes so I can report what really happened. And so I know he's all right. When he didn't make our initial rendezvous and Carl was reported dead, I was worried. Especially with those awful articles popping up."

Elinor nodded. "I'm sorry I didn't tell you from the start. I didn't know what had happened, so I didn't know if I could trust you. I was trying to protect my brother."

"Understandable. Had I realized you were his sister, I would have come right out and told you the details. But I didn't know I could trust you either."

They exchanged smiles.

"Well." She didn't know what else to say, even as she wished they could just sit and talk. Not about criminals and marshal business, but about why he found himself yearning for a quieter life, how she'd found that here, what he imagined for his future.

"Perhaps..." She stopped before the question escaped. Would it be too forward? If so, he could simply ignore her request. She lifted her chin. "Perhaps you could write to me? Let me know how everything goes in Nashville, and when you get back to Chicago."

She expected a dismissal, maybe even narrowed eyes or an outright refusal to share information she had no right to.

He nodded, smiling again. "I'd like that. And maybe..." He paused, cleared his throat. "I'm thinking I'd like to come down this way again sometime when I can better enjoy it. Perhaps I could stop by to say hello. See how Judah is doing."

"You'd be welcome." Did she say it too quickly? Gracious, she felt like a schoolgirl again instead of a widowed woman of twenty-eight. "Perhaps next time you'll accept that invitation for dinner."

"It would be my—"

But he never finished what he was about to say. Shouts rent the air from behind the house, and then worse—gunshots. Three of them, all tumbling over each other. She jolted, spun, and might have tried to convince herself it was just a neighbor out hunting, but she couldn't.

Not when she heard the unmistakable sound of Judah's scream.

Chapter Seventeen

Hannah drove back to the Payne house just before noon on Sunday, glad she'd been able to rest and attend church that morning but also feeling a little bad for leaving the crew to fend for themselves for breakfast. They had insisted they'd be fine—and there had been plenty of leftovers from the last few days—but still.

Kayla and Ryan had joined her for church, and it had been fun to introduce them to her friends there. Though they hadn't lingered long afterward. With only a few more days left to solve the mystery and the sun peeking through the clouds, she knew they were eager to get back outside.

She flicked on her blinker and turned into the long driveway, a glance in her rearview mirror showing her another car close behind her.

That was odd. It wasn't Ford's car, nor Brooke's Suburban. But she'd just seen it yesterday—at the library.

Apparently, Mrs. Bryant and Kayla had managed to set up a meeting. But what information could the elderly woman have?

Hannah avoided the potholes as best as she could while her mind went over the possibilities. She hadn't seen much of her former teacher since middle school, but clearly she was a regular at Neil's store, so she must still come to Blackberry Valley often. Did Mrs. Bryant have some reason to be interested in the story? And if so, was it a benevolent interest? Or one that could lead her to cause trouble?

She shook her head at herself. Too many unexplained events recently had made her paranoid. Why else would she suspect Mrs. Bryant of anything other than wanting to be helpful?

Hannah parked in her usual spot. The crew were all in the yard, conferring about something with wide arm gestures. Oran had the drone in his hands, so she assumed the discussion was about where to send it.

Mrs. Bryant pulled in alongside Hannah and got out with a grin and a wave. "Hello again, Hannah."

"Hi, Mrs. Bryant." She knew her confusion colored her tone and was likely on her face. She glanced down, trying to get a gauge on the woman's shoes. Larger than her own, but with more tread than the footprints, from what she could see. Though, of course, she must own more than one pair.

Ryan strode toward them with an enthusiastic wave. "You must be Rhiannon."

Mrs. Bryant nodded and moved to intercept Ryan with an outstretched hand. "So good to meet you, Ryan. Thanks for inviting me out here. It's been years since I've seen the place."

Ryan looked puzzled. "You know the house?"

"Oh sure. We all came here for holidays when Uncle Judah was still alive."

"Uncle Judah," Hannah repeated. "Wait. You and Ford are related?"

"Technically Judah was my great-great-uncle, but yeah." She frowned. "Though when he died, it was as if the Payne side of the family decided we didn't exist anymore. No more invitations, no more family reunions. And all because of the newspaper article Ford's dad found."

"Wait, wait, wait. I need to know what this article is," Ryan said. "But let's get the cameras rolling first. Kayla should be coming with the release form any second."

Kayla must have detoured into the house, because she came out the front door, clipboard and pen in hand and a smile on her face. While Mrs. Bryant read and signed, Kayla turned to Ryan. "I'm thinking inside for this, yeah? If she has papers."

"Do I ever." Mrs. Bryant finished signing with a flourish and handed the clipboard back to Kayla. She patted the bag slung over her shoulder. "And yes, please. I've been dying to see what Ford and Denise did to the place. They didn't take out Uncle Judah's rock collection, did they? If so, I really don't know what I'll do."

"The rock collection is still intact," Ryan assured her. He turned to the yard and waved to the crew. "Change of plans, everyone. Rhiannon was able to make it earlier after all. Let's do that interview while Hannah works on lunch, and then we'll do the drone work after."

"Ford will be fit to be tied when he hears I'm out here," Mrs. Bryant said with a laugh.

Family feuds were weird—and it was weirder still to think of her former teacher being part of one. Hannah shook her head and let herself be ushered with the others through the front door. Then she slipped off to the kitchen.

Lunch today was simply chips, veggies, and sandwiches on fresh French bread she'd prepped overnight and baked at home this morning, so it wouldn't take long to get ready. That had been her plan, knowing she wouldn't be there all morning. Still, she couldn't quite justify leaving it so she could go hear what Mrs. Bryant was saying, even though curiosity had her straining her ears.

She smiled when she heard Trevor say, "The lighting's way better in the kitchen, with all the windows. And the table gives us more options for spreading things out but still seeing you both."

A moment later Kayla appeared. "Would we bother you if we filmed in here?"

Hannah shot her a knowing look. "Do you really have to ask? I'm dying of curiosity."

Kayla laughed, then glanced at the things Hannah had out on the counter. "I guess what I should be asking is if you can either pause your prep or do it quietly."

"It's just sandwiches. I'll get everything opened before you start rolling and do the quiet stuff during."

"Perfect." Kayla called everyone in, and Hannah made good on her word, getting everything out of the fridge that she'd need and taking it all out of noisy wrappings.

Mrs. Bryant gaped as she came in. "Gracious. Denise sure went to town in here, didn't she? What a beautiful space."

Hannah continued to work while the crew set up lights and positioned Ryan and their guest. Kayla clapped them in with the slate.

"So I'm here now with another side of the Payne family," Ryan said. "Rhiannon Bryant, right?" He held out a hand.

She shook. "That's right. Though my maiden name is Davis."

Ryan nodded. "Uh-huh. And tell me how the Davis family is related to the Paynes."

"My great-grandfather, Frank Davis, was Judah Payne's half-brother."

"Wait, Frank? Is that a coincidence?"

Hannah glanced up and saw Mrs. Bryant grin. "Not at all. He was named after Franklin Sullivan, Judah's uncle, who died saving him. Judah's mother, Elinor, remarried two years after her brother's death. To Franklin's partner in the US Marshals, Nathan Davis."

Hannah looked up again. Ryan wore an expression that was equal parts surprise and delight. "Whoa. Back up. Franklin Sullivan was…?"

Mrs. Bryant smiled. "Working undercover with the marshals."

"And you know this how? Because when I spoke with your cousin, he said Sullivan was an outlaw. The black sheep of the family."

Mrs. Bryant snorted. "Well, Ford never was very good at research—always in too much of a rush. No offense to him. But I can prove that Franklin was a lawman, not an outlaw."

Ryan nodded again. "Okay. Let's see it."

Kayla stopped the filming, and they moved to the table. Hannah focused on her sandwiches while Mrs. Bryant unloaded her bag. Kayla murmured instructions about setting it all out in an orderly fashion, and then she let Ryan lead Mrs. Bryant through explanations.

Hannah looked at the supplies she had out and made a face. "Can I grab something from the pantry real quick?"

"Sure," Kayla said.

Not wanting to delay them any more than necessary, Hannah hurried into the pantry where she'd stashed the paper supplies and nonperishable food. She grabbed the can of sun-dried tomatoes she needed, then thought she might as well carry out the chips, crackers, and paper plates as well.

On second thought, maybe not. She fumbled the plates and nearly dropped the bag of chips when she bent to pick them up. She reached for the pack of plates that had fallen into the same box the utensils and coffee filters had been hidden in—and paused. The light from the kitchen reached in and caught on something beside the box. She set the tomatoes down to see what could be glinting like that.

It felt like a smooth stone—maybe a gemstone? She held it up to the light and could see that it was blue, about two inches long. Maybe a crystal of some kind? Not exactly odd around this house. It could have simply broken off from a piece of something.

But what was that at the top?

Needing better light, she gathered her supplies again and stood, moving back to the kitchen before her precarious heap tumbled again. Seeing that Kayla was writing something down, Hannah first hurried to open the jar and get the noisy chip bags into place on the counter, then turned her attention once again to the crystal.

Definitely not just broken off something. It had a loop at one end, the kind used to attach things to jewelry.

She opened her mouth to ask the crew if anyone had lost any-thing but then changed her mind. Aside from Lexi's wedding rings, neither she nor Kayla wore any jewelry, and Hannah didn't need to ask why, given the way Brooke had had to take hers off.

And besides, this stone was too big to be from a bracelet and didn't have the sort of decorative metalwork that made her think it was part of a necklace. Just a utilitarian loop.

What else could it be from?

"Hold on," Kayla said, pulling Hannah's attention away from the stone for a moment. "Let me grab my laptop from my room." She pulled a key out of her pocket and jogged away.

Key. Keychain—that could be what this blue crystal was from. And it had been where the missing kitchen items were hidden.

Which meant it could have fallen from the keychain of whoever had stashed them there.

From what she'd seen, the bedroom keys weren't on keychains, nor were the extra house keys the crew had been using. And the only other keys she'd seen anyone with were to the vehicles, which both had the plastic tab with the rental agency's logo on it.

Not the crew then. Which didn't surprise her. And this definitely had not been in the pantry when she'd first loaded her boxes and supplies in there. There was no way she would have missed it on the otherwise empty shelving and floors.

"Okay, I'm back," Kayla said, entering with her laptop open and balanced in one arm, tapping at the keys with the other. "Looks like Judah died in 1984 at the age of seventy-nine. That sound right?"

Mrs. Bryant nodded. "Yes, that's right."

Kayla slid the computer on the counter and reached for the slate. "Okay. Are we good?"

"Let's go," Ryan said.

Hannah fished a few of the sun-dried tomatoes from the jar and positioned them on her small cutting board. Thanks to years of practice, she could cut without letting her knife clatter against the board. The only noise was from the slate.

"Okay, Rhiannon, show me what we're looking at here."

"Well, Ryan, this is a Certificate of Valor from the US Marshal Service."

"Seriously?" Ryan's grin was audible.

Mrs. Bryant laughed. "Seriously. You can see that this is an official document recognizing the courage shown by Franklin Sullivan on April 14, 1910, when he died in the line of duty."

A page rustled. "Yeah, it says that right here. So if we know Sullivan was a marshal, why all the confusion about how he died?"

Mrs. Bryant sighed. "Well, that's the thing. Apparently, in order to protect Franklin's sister and her son, Franklin's partner Nathan leaked a false story to the reporter who'd already written about Franklin being on the run from the law, in order to throw the remaining anarchists off the scent. His goal was clearly to keep Elinor and Judah safe, given that Franklin was shot right here."

Hannah looked up and saw that Ryan's eyes were wide. "Right here—as in, here in the kitchen?"

"No, no." Mrs. Bryant turned to the bank of windows and motioned toward the backyard. "Right out there, between the house and the trees."

"But how do you know all of this? The owner of the house didn't seem to."

Hannah wondered if they'd cut the roll of Mrs. Bryant's eyes from the final edit. "That's because Ford and his father won't listen to anything I have to say. Ford's father, Ron, went berserk when he found a copy of an old article that cited Nathan Davis as the lawman who shot Franklin. It was right after Judah died, and Ron was understandably raw. But when he saw that, he declared the Davis side of the family to be a bunch of backstabbing opportunists and cut us all off."

"So when did you find these papers?" Ryan asked.

"When I found out you and your film crew were in town and what you were here for, I thought it was important to look again for any information I could find. All of this was in the attic in a box that's been overlooked for many years."

The front door opened and then slammed shut.

"Hold up," Kayla called, looking more frustrated than curious as to who had let themselves in.

Hannah checked her watch. It wouldn't be Lacy—she'd promised to have lunch with her mom today. And Dad and Uncle Gordon wouldn't be coming until four.

Ford Payne burst into the kitchen, fury on his face. "What is *she* doing here?" He pointed at Mrs. Bryant.

She straightened her spine and lifted her chin. "I was *invited*, thank you very much."

"I told you forty years ago you weren't welcome here, and that hasn't changed."

"Oh, for crying out loud, Ford. Don't be so foolish. I'm clearing the name of the uncle you've always been too embarrassed to claim, so I'm doing *you* a favor."

Trevor and Oran both repositioned themselves and kept their cameras up, and Lexi fiddled with her dials, a smirk lurking in the corners of her mouth.

Well, drama made good television, Hannah supposed. She gave up on the food and turned to watch it unfold.

Ford had gone red in the face. "If it's foolish to be upset that your ancestor killed mine, then I'll be a fool."

"You see?" Mrs. Bryant said to Ryan, who had his lips sealed. She waved a hand toward Ford. "Too stubborn to even hear straight. Listen, Ford. Here are the facts. My ancestor did not shoot your ancestor. Franklin Sullivan wasn't an outlaw. He didn't steal a diamond, and he didn't murder a man. He was a US Marshal."

"He was what?" Ford deflated before their eyes, blinking rapidly. "Did you say a marshal?"

Mrs. Bryant picked up the Certificate of Valor and shook it. "Like I said, he didn't steal that diamond. He went undercover to get it back. Carl Parson, the anarchist who actually stole it, was onto Frank and took a shot at him. Franklin shot back to defend himself, and Parson was killed."

Ford stared at her. "So…"

"So it was self-defense. Then a few weeks later, he was shot and killed by one of Carl Parson's brothers."

Ford's expression shuttered again. "But Nathan Davis was named in the article Dad found as the one who shot him."

"That's what Nathan told the press to protect Elinor and Judah. When the Parson brothers came out of the woods that day, they were pointing their guns at Judah. They were yelling about killing him to punish Franklin for turning on them. That was their way. Franklin shot them both but not before one of them got a shot off at him. Nathan was afraid their cousins would come after Judah if they realized he was Franklin's nephew and that Franklin had shot all three brothers, so he planted the story that he and his fellow marshals tracked Franklin and the two remaining Parson brothers down and killed them. If the Parson family knew the truth about him being undercover, there's no way that gang would have let it rest."

Ford shook his head. "You can't know that. It's a great story, but—"

"I've got the transcripts from the official report, Ford." Mrs. Bryant pulled a few more sheets from her folder. "Depositions not only from Nathan Davis, but from Elinor and Judah Payne. This anger you and your dad have held on to for forty years, the contempt for the whole Davis line—it's based on a cover-up meant to deceive criminals, not on the truth."

Ford sagged against the table, something clattering against the wood as his hand came to a rest. His keys.

Hannah edged closer, studying the bits she could see. It wasn't much until he lifted his hand to rub at his temple. Then she saw what she'd suspected. There was a dangling chain with no charm attached. Her focus dropped to his shoes—dress shoes, like the ones he'd worn that first day. Not overly large for a man's foot, but bigger than hers for sure.

And he'd known when Brooke was at the house, had seen her vehicle…but how? He must have driven down the driveway to see that. Then the doorbell camera. He'd never given them the videos, just assured them there'd been nothing on them at the times in question.

Of course he'd say that, because it would have recorded *him*. He obviously had a key to the house, since he owned the place. And with the camera footage, he could have easily kept track of their comings and goings.

"You tried to scare off the crew." She didn't mean to say it out loud, but it came out, and the cameras swung her way. She stepped out from behind the island, crystal key fob in hand. "This was in the pantry, where you hid my utensils and coffee filters. And your footprints were in the yard, even though you allegedly haven't been here since that first day. But you knew your daughter was here—and you weren't happy about her helping, I assume."

Ford had the grace to look sheepish. "I heard one of the crew talking about ghosts. He sounded frightened by the idea, so I thought it would convince him to leave, and the rest with him. I didn't want to cause any harm or real trouble. I wanted you all to decide the story wasn't worth the hassle."

Ryan snorted a laugh. "Clearly, you've never watched my first show—*Uncover the Unknown*, in which we actively hunted for ghosts. Convincing us Franklin Sullivan haunted the place only would have whetted our appetite, not scared us off."

"Not that we were convinced," Kayla chimed in.

Lexi took off her headphones. "One question though. My toothbrush?"

Ford frowned. "I didn't touch anybody's toothbrush."

Oran's shoulders shook with laughter as Lexi spun on him. "You!"

Oran lowered his camera. "That was the only thing I did. I promise. I wouldn't ever cause problems for the show—but come on. You were being unreasonable."

Lexi considered for a moment, then smiled. "Fair enough. Truce?"

"Truce." He raised his camera again.

Kayla stepped closer. "So the relocated stuff, the email to Hannah, the note on the laptop, the voice in the cave—that was all you?"

He nodded to most of the accusations, but frowned at the last. "What cave?"

"You expect us to believe you don't know about the cave?" Ryan asked.

Mrs. Bryant snorted. "Believe it. He's never been one to go outside exploring. Brooke knew though. I'm the one who told her where to find it." She grinned. "Her father tried to keep her out of my class, but the school board wasn't having any of his ridiculous feud. When we got to the geology unit, I happened to mention the cave my cousins and I discovered near my uncle Judah's place. I knew she'd come asking about it, and sure enough, she was waiting for me after class. Good girl, that daughter of yours. She knows family's more important than any tired old feud."

Ford looked as though he couldn't decide whether to be distressed or flattered.

Ryan frowned. "So the tinware in there wasn't actually old, then. You planted it."

Mrs. Bryant shook her head. "No, that's real. When Judah showed us the cave, he told us not to take anything from it and not to leave anything there. It was a memorial to his uncle, a way to remember the sacrifice he made. The only thing he and his mother took out was a Bible she'd loaned to Franklin. It had belonged to Judah's father, so they didn't want to risk it being damaged."

Ryan nodded, face serious. "We took the tinware out to get photos and look it up, but we'll put it all back."

Mrs. Bryant shrugged. "You can, but now that Cody owns it, he gets the final say, I guess. Last I heard, that boy thought he could charge people to come see it. As if it's big enough to be a tourist attraction. I tried to tell him it was silly, but he insisted."

"You know Cody Coleman?" Kayla asked.

"Oh, sure. I introduced myself when he moved to town and bought the property. I showed him the cave, hoping to instill in him the importance of preserving the legacy it represented." She screwed up her face. "That was a misjudgment on my part. He might never have found it if I hadn't opened my big mouth."

Ryan looked at Kayla. "Are you thinking what I'm thinking?"

Kayla folded her arms over her chest. "That Cody got Hannah's message as soon as she sent it but didn't reply until he'd had a chance to set up some sort of audio player? Yes, that's exactly what I'm thinking."

"If he wants to profit off the cave, his best shot is probably to tell Franklin's story. All the better if he could claim Franklin was haunting the place." Ryan shook his head. "How convenient of us to come to town and want to film there. Cody probably hoped we'd be free marketing and promotion for his amazing haunted cave."

"One way to find out." Kayla strode toward the mudroom. "Who's up for a hike?"

"It's probably still pretty wet in there, Kay," Ryan warned.

She peered over her shoulder and met his gaze. "So let's be careful."

It was all the permission the crew needed. Hannah figured it was safe to assume no one would want sandwiches until they got back from the cave, so she wrapped up what she'd done so far and put everything in the fridge. No way was she missing this.

Her phone buzzed in her pocket as she reached for her jacket. It was Lacy. HEY, MOM AND I ARE DONE SO I THOUGHT I'D SWING OUT TO HELP WITH LUNCH CLEANUP, BUT THERE ARE EXTRA CARS OUT HERE. WHAT'S GOING ON? DO I DARE COME IN?

Hannah grinned and swiped a response. WE'RE HEADING TO THE CAVE. MEET US AT THE KITCHEN DOOR. HOPE YOU'RE WEARING YOUR BOOTS!

The reply came in before Hannah returned her phone to her pocket. ALWAYS!

Once outside, Kayla shoved wearable cameras at Hannah and Lacy. "I know, I know, you're demoted to support staff again. Rhiannon actually makes more sense as a guide—sorry."

Hannah laughed. "Are we seriously refilming this for a third time?"

"Probably, but not today. We've only got a brief window before the rain moves in again, so let's just get back to the cave and see what we can find." Kayla darted to the front of the group. "Don't worry about filming the walk-up in any organized way. Let's just get there. My radar says forty-five minutes before the next storm rolls in. We need to get a move on."

Hannah slid her camera into its holster so she could hurry after the crew. Through the woods, over the stream, then the squeeze into the cave. She barely had time to get nervous about the cramped space.

They'd no sooner splashed their way into the inch-deep water on the downhill side of the main chamber than Lexi called out, "Quiet!"

The group went still, and Hannah immediately heard what had grabbed Lexi's attention. The moaning they'd heard before tapered off. Then the whispers started.

Lexi pointed to the rock wall between the main chamber and the one Franklin had stayed in. "It's coming from somewhere over there. And it's definitely a recording. This is the exact track I analyzed. Yep, there's the dog barking."

Hannah still hadn't heard that, but she didn't have the tools Lexi did to amplify things. They hurried to the wall and ran their hands over any ledge or crevice they could find. Hannah paused when another sound came, this one from directly above where she stood. "It's here, but I can't reach it." She could see a ledge above her, but strain as she might, it remained a few inches above her fingers.

Ryan came over and swiped a hand over the shelf—coming back with a white MP3 player. "Found it," he called.

Oran sighed. "Bummer. Not a ghost."

Lexi laughed and nudged his shoulder. "Not this time. But that doesn't mean you didn't experience something truly bizarre in Transylvania."

He grinned at her. "If you keep talking like that, your toothbrush will always be safe from me."

Everyone crowded around Ryan. "Not that it's really much of a mystery, but let's see if we can identify the owner." He pressed a few buttons. "Looks like it was looping tracks forty through forty-three. Other tracks include 'Tell Me I'm Somebody,' 'Small Town Hometown,' 'Back Yonder'—"

"Those are the songs on the demo Cody gave me," Hannah said. "I saw the titles when I found the card." And why in the world hadn't he taken the time to delete his own songs before he hid the player? He must have been in a hurry.

"Well, it seems our ghosts have been busted." Ryan cracked a smile at the camera. "Did you get that? That's gold."

Kayla rolled her eyes and gestured to Mrs. Bryant and Ford. "Aren't you forgetting something?"

"Oh, right." Shooing the rest of them back, Ryan moved to the cousins. "You guys up for a peek at Franklin's hideout? I'd love your insight on the map."

"Map?" Mrs. Bryant frowned. "What map?"

They moved into the smaller chamber and situated lights, but Mrs. Bryant still shook her head when Ryan pointed to the lines and X. "I never saw that as a map. Are you sure?"

"No. It's a working theory." Ryan turned his gaze on Lacy. "Hopefully Neil can help us with it."

Chapter Eighteen

Poring over maps for hours on end had become dull. Hannah and Lacy left Ryan and Neil and the crew to it and escaped onto the street to breathe in the crisp air of the spring morning. She'd been a bit surprised that Ryan had stuck to his resolution not to interrupt Neil's Sunday afternoon, but she was quickly learning that what looked like immediate moves on his show often spanned days or even weeks. And happened out of order.

It turned out that filming required way more patience than she had ever expected. But they'd put their Sunday afternoon to good use by planning out the reenactment portion of the show—and recruiting local talent. Hannah's brother Drew would be Franklin, and his wife Allison would be Elinor. Their son Axel would play Judah. Given that they weren't speaking roles, all three had been happy to agree. Kayla had been chasing down costuming since then. They'd shoot those scenes tomorrow, when the sun was scheduled to reappear.

Lacy stretched her back, as she did frequently now that she carried more weight in the front. "Have they gone through all the stuff Mrs. Bryant left them yet?" She'd met them at the bookstore that morning. Breakfast had been a simple overnight French toast casserole, so Hannah hadn't needed any help.

"When I came in this morning, the table was still covered with the photographs she gave them to go through, and what Phyllis had lent us too. I think that's what most of them did yesterday after she and Ford left." Hannah had given the photos a cursory glance but hadn't had the chance to study them. "Well, other than calling Cody Coleman and confronting him. On speakerphone. That was fun. Dad and Uncle Gordon were highly entertained."

Lacy meandered toward a bench. "Did he fess up?"

"In about two seconds." Trying to fake his way onto TV wasn't exactly a great idea, but it was still less creepy than Ford Payne letting himself into the rental house to try to scare them. Ryan and the crew had taken it in stride, but Hannah wouldn't be recommending the rental to any friends who came to town, that was for sure. She was glad he and Mrs. Bryant had made peace though.

"And I guess Jada was trying to claw her way up the show-biz ladder." Lacy sat with a happy sigh, stretching out her legs.

"I guess." Hannah started to take a seat beside her but paused when Liam's Jeep pulled into a parking spot. Her heart rate kicked up a notch. Silly? Maybe. But she hadn't expected to see him that morning, and the opportunity made her smile. "Hey," she called when he stepped out of his Jeep.

His grin lit up his face. "Hey, yourself." He strode over to them and greeted her with a kiss. "You still meeting Raquel soon?"

She checked her watch. "In ten minutes. I left her gifts with their hosts last night."

"Any idea what time you'll be done? I thought I'd go out to the Payne place after lunch with Ryan before I have to get to work. Get a little time with you, anyway."

She slipped an arm around his waist. He didn't take night shifts often, and when she was at the restaurant until closing, she barely noticed them. But this week she had. "Raquel's surprise date via video chat is actually a lunch date, because that was how their schedules worked out. The crew just wanted leftovers for lunch, so I figured I'd come out afterward, clean up whatever they empty, and get some of the dinner prep done."

"Good. I'll see you there, then."

Ryan emerged from the bookshop, hand raised in greeting. "Liam, my man. Right on time."

Liam gave her another kiss and stepped away. "See you in a bit."

"Hey, wait a minute. The maps? Any luck?"

Ryan made a face. "We tried it every which way, but the only thing that made any sense was that it's a map from the cave to the house. So not a treasure map. Just directions back to his sister's place, no doubt so he wouldn't get lost in the dark."

"Well, that's anticlimactic," Lacy said.

"I know, right?" He grinned. "I need some good wings to cheer me up. Lead on, Liam."

"Have fun." Hannah waved them off and then turned to Lacy. "Guess I'd better meet Raquel. See you after lunch?"

"You got it."

Raquel had suggested meeting at the Hot Spot, but knowing Jacob was already there getting Raquel's surprise lunch started, Hannah had instead suggested they meet outside Jump Start Coffee. It was their first stop anyway. Hannah arrived first, but she'd only been there a minute when Raquel walked up.

"Hi," Hannah said. "Does the new plan sound okay?" She'd figured she better make sure Raquel wore appropriate clothes for their walk around town, so she'd suggested a quick bite at the café and then a bit of shopping.

"Sure." Raquel moved toward the door, holding it open to let Hannah go in first.

As soon as she entered, Hannah made eye contact with Zane, who smiled and nodded.

"Not sure what I'm in the mood for today." Raquel hung back, eyes on the menu board behind the counter.

Given the lack of line—she couldn't remember the last time that had happened—Hannah urged her forward. "Let's ask Zane what's good today." Once they were close enough, she said, "Hey, Zane. Any recommendations?"

"As a matter of fact, I recommend a stroll down memory lane." He reached under the counter and came up with a bouquet of red roses, which he held out to Raquel. "From Marshall."

"Oh my goodness." Raquel took the roses, eyes wide. "Marshall sent these here?"

Hannah laughed. "He's arranged a tour for you. I'm playing guide in his absence. This is stop one, because this is where you had your first date, six months ago."

Zane grinned and held out two lidded cups. "And a little latte to hold you both over. On the house."

"Aw, thanks." Hannah took her cup, and Raquel shifted the roses to one arm so she could take the other. "Ready for the next stop?"

A little misty-eyed, Raquel nodded.

They collected teal and silver balloons to commemorate the surprise party Marshall had arranged for Raquel before he took the job in Chicago, a snow globe with ice skaters inside to remember their ice-skating date, and a gorgeous charm bracelet with six charms on it, one for each month they'd been together. The last of the gifts that Marshall had shipped was a box of Raquel's favorite gourmet chocolates, but Hannah stopped her before she could open it.

"We have one more stop." They'd circled their way around downtown and were back in view of the Hot Spot.

Raquel's smile had been nonstop since Zane had revealed the roses. Hannah had to imagine that even her cheerful waitress's face was beginning to hurt. "Let me guess—you're putting me to work?"

"You know it." Hannah pulled out her key to unlock the front door, then marveled along with Raquel at what Jacob and Elaine had done to get the place ready. The lighting was low, the tables pushed back against the walls—all except one two-top, which they'd draped with a red tablecloth. A candle burned in the center, and soft music filled the room from the speakers.

"This is beautiful," Raquel whispered. Then she frowned at the table. It only had one chair. On the table at the second place setting was an open laptop computer.

"Sit," Hannah said.

Raquel sat, and when she did, her face lit up. "Marshall!"

Hannah edged into view enough to wave at him.

Marshall wore his brightest smile. "Hey, beautiful. Sorry I couldn't be there, but I still wanted to spend the day with you. So Jacob has prepared you a meal, and I have one here." He lifted his plate enough to catch it on camera. "So we can be together, even if we're not together."

"Aw, Marshall." Raquel clasped her hands together. "This is so sweet."

And that was Hannah's cue to leave. She waved goodbye and slid the gifts she'd carried onto one of the empty tables, then made her exit, glad she could play a part in this, however small.

She thought she might beat Liam and Ryan back to the Payne farm, but they were just climbing out of Liam's Jeep when she pulled in. *Perfect.* And even better, they both seemed to be in high spirits, given their grins and laughter.

Liam waited for her, though Ryan had gone inside by the time she parked and got out. "Hello again," he said. "How did the surprise go?"

"Great. How was lunch?" She slipped her hand into the crook of his elbow.

"Enlightening."

"Well, that's cryptic. How so?"

Liam was grinning, so it couldn't be anything bad. "Let's just say my hunch was right on the money."

It took her a second, but then her eyes went wide. "You mean he admitted he's got a thing for Kayla?"

Liam nodded.

"And he confessed it to you? A near-stranger?"

He chuckled. "He asked for advice on how to get out of the friend zone. Apparently, Kayla told him you and I were friends first and then started dating."

"Sure, but they've been in the friend zone for forever. We were only there for a couple of months. Not that you wouldn't have good advice." She grinned, lifting her brows. "I hope."

"We'll see. I did let him know our situation was different. But I also told him to tell her how he feels."

"Simple. Straightforward." She made a show of considering. "It'll do. I might have suggested a grand gesture, a romantic kiss, something dramatic. But then, they have plenty of drama."

Liam laughed and led her through the door.

They found the crew gathered around the kitchen table, a discarded dessert plate beside each of them. The photos from Mrs. Bryant's collection were spread out before them. Lacy was in Hannah's usual place beside Kayla, flipping through a few papers.

Ryan leaned over his spot at the head of the table but didn't sit. He glanced at Liam and nodded once.

Clearly some cue from their conversation, since Liam smiled. An encouragement? Surely he wasn't telling Ryan to declare his feelings here and now, in front of everyone, right? She couldn't believe that was what Kayla would want.

But Ryan went back to the photos. He reached out and tapped one. "Something about these keep drawing me."

"Judah's rock collection?" Kayla leaned forward. "What about them? I mean, they're in black and white, so it's hard to tell what's what."

"Yeah, but this one. See that label?" He leaned closer and pointed to something written on the box in the photo. "'From Uncle Franklin.'"

Hannah leaned in for a closer look. The collection spanned several photographs—not a huge surprise given that there were many examples of it in every single room of the house—but the box with that label was huge. It had all sorts of geology samples, many of which she didn't even have names for. She recognized some crystals and geodes and what might be amber, but the rest? She had no idea.

Then her eyes tracked back to the crystals. There were quite a number of them, and the varying shades of white and gray in the photo made her think they were probably various colors. But one looked different. She grabbed Ryan's arm. "Ryan, is that the diamond?"

Ryan frowned down at the photo, then his eyes went wide. "If so, then..."

Hannah laughed. "Then the diamond is here. Which means it *was* a map back to the house, yes—but not because he couldn't find his way otherwise. Because this was where he left the diamond. With Judah in his rock collection. You heard what Rhiannon said. He frequently sent Judah things for his collection. Crystals, geodes, fossils, meteors. No one would think anything of it. They'd assume it was another stone in a little boy's collection."

Ryan frowned. "But Judah went on to become a professor of geology, and he obviously handled each piece as he worked it into this place. You think he didn't realize what it was?"

Hannah grinned. "On the contrary. I think he knew *exactly* what it was. And I think he realized his uncle died securing it, and so he went on keeping it secure. I think he put it in this house to keep it safe." She spun, eyes scanning over the stones worked into the kitchen. "Let's get looking."

Ryan grinned and clapped his hands together. "Cameras up! Let's find a diamond."

Chapter Nineteen

Elinor leaned against the doorframe and found Judah in his usual spot—on the rug in front of his window with his box of geological treasures in front of him. Nothing unusual, but these last two months, it seemed he only cared about the pieces Franklin had found for him. Every time she came up, he was examining one of the last pieces her brother had brought for him on that disastrous trip.

Her chest ached. "Morning, baby," she whispered into the room. "Happy birthday."

Judah looked up and gave her a smile. But it wasn't as bright as it had once been. She couldn't blame him for that. It had been a hard two months, especially for him. First the horror of seeing someone aim a gun at him, then the trauma of his uncle dying before his eyes, protecting him. Then the secretive trip to Chicago for

235

the funeral, all while newspapers ran the fake story Nathan had devised.

To keep them safe. She knew that. Appreciated it. Had agreed to it.

But it hadn't stopped her old neighbors from murmuring, judging, and condemning. Her stomach rolled at the idea of her noble brother's reputation being destroyed forever.

It was better here in Blackberry Valley. If anyone had seen the article, they didn't say as much to her. If anyone knew the events had happened right outside of town, they pretended not to.

She still dreamed of it, all too often. She knew Judah did too. Maybe they always would.

But it was time to live their lives. Celebrate their milestones. That was what Franklin would have wanted.

She pushed herself off the doorframe and held out a hand. "Ready for breakfast? I'm making pancakes. Your favorite."

"Thank you, Mama." He didn't get up immediately. First, he lifted the crystal he held and gave it a kiss. "Thank you, Uncle Franklin," he whispered.

For a moment, the light caught the stone just so and sent a rainbow across the floor before he put it back in the box. She smiled. A gift from her brother, from heaven. A rainbow—a promise.

Judah scrambled up, took her hand, and led her down the stairs. Both of them stopped when a shadow moved at the window in the front door. It was too early for callers. Surely it wasn't one of the Parson cousins Nathan had warned her about. It couldn't be.

A knock. Would a criminal knock? Then a voice. "I know it's early. I'm sorry. I rode through the night because I couldn't be late for Judah's birthday."

"Nathan!" Judah sprang forward before she could, unlocked the door, and threw it open. In the next moment, he'd tossed himself at Nathan Davis's legs, and the marshal—former marshal, if he was back here—lifted him with a laugh.

Elinor moved more slowly but with no less joy in her soul. Her eyes met Nathan's over Judah's head. Those kind blue eyes, so full, so trustworthy.

He'd said he'd return, promised it at the end of every letter, every week. He poured out his heart, how he'd long feared he'd meet his end in his work, and how he had, that day Franklin had died. Just not the way he'd expected. How he'd known it was time to retire from the Marshals and find a new calling— and how every time he prayed about it, the only place he could think of was here.

She poured out her own heart in response. Her grief, her loneliness, her longing for a new beginning.

And there he was. Her new beginning. She leaned into the doorway and let a smile curve her lips. "Well, Mr. Davis. You're a bit early for dinner, but come on in. I was about to make pancakes."

"My favorite," he said.

Judah's eyes sparkled up at him. "Mine too."

Hannah had yet to see the upstairs of the house, but she somehow ended up there now, a flashlight in hand to shine at any crystals that needed investigating. The cameras were running, which meant the only ones actively searching with her were Liam, Lacy, Kayla, and Ryan. And they had their marching orders, of course. Whoever spotted it first would call for Ryan, and the camera crew would follow.

It was his show, after all.

She and Liam finished scouring the hall and turned into the bedroom that, according to the photographs, had been Judah's as a boy, and he'd kept it as his own even when he became the master of the house decades later. He shared it, for a time, with his half brother, while their three sisters had been in the one next to theirs.

"You take left, I'll take right, and we meet in the middle again?" Liam suggested.

"Sounds like a plan." Her phone buzzed in her pocket. Lacy texted that they'd come up empty in the living room. Hannah set her phone on the dresser and followed the lines of the room, gaze sweeping over every rock, every geode, every crystal. Whenever she saw a white one, she flashed her light at it, but no rainbows.

Until she got to the second wall, halfway along it, right above the four-poster bed. This time, when she directed the beam of her flashlight up, rainbows leaped out. And her heart leaped into her throat. "Liam! Ryan! Up here!"

Liam was at her side in a heartbeat, laughing. Seconds later, a stampede sounded on the stairs, and then the room swarmed with people.

Hannah pointed up. "There. Look." She flashed the beam again, and rainbows danced.

Ryan wasted no time. He jumped onto the bed, and between that and his height, had no problem reaching the place where the diamond was worked into the molding.

"Careful," Kayla said, though softly enough not to be picked up by Lexi's mic.

Ryan shot a grin at her. "It's a diamond, Kay. The hardest natural substance on the planet. I'm not going to hurt it." He ran his fingers over it, then said, "We need to contact Ford and get his reaction on camera also. We cracked the case, you guys!"

Whoops sounded from the crew, and Hannah joined in. At least until Liam pressed something into her hand. "Wanna get a photo?"

He'd given her her phone, which she'd left on the dresser. "Thanks." She woke up the screen and prepared to tap her camera icon, but a screen was open—her contacts. Smiling, she looked to see what Liam had renamed himself this time.

Her heart stuttered. Where it had said *Liam "My Love" Berthold* this morning, it now read, *Liam "Your Fiancé?" Berthold*.

"What?" She spun.

Liam was on one knee, already reaching for her hand.

She gave it to him, trembling.

"Hannah," he said. "I wanted to find a quiet time to ask you this. But then I realized we seem to run from one adventure to the next, and if I wait for quiet, we'll be waiting forever. So I decided to just take the next opportunity to ask if I can share in your adventures as your husband, and if you'll share in mine as my wife. Will you marry me?"

"Liam." She'd thought her heart raced before, but now it galloped. And while she knew the only word that mattered, she was too excited to voice it. So she held up a finger, pulled her hand free, made a quick edit to his contact, then turned the phone around.

Liam grinned. His contact now read, *Liam "My Fiancé!" Berthold*. He laughed, stood, and scooped her into a hug as the room erupted into cheers once more. Lacy barely waited until Hannah's feet were back on the ground before she swooped in for a hug of her own.

"Hey, Liam." They both looked over at Ryan, who still stood on the bed with the diamond in his hand. He made as if to throw it. "You forgot something."

Liam laughed and shook his head. "No, I didn't." He reached into his pocket and took out a little velvet bag. A moment later, he shook a ring into his palm.

A white-gold filigree surrounded a beautiful round diamond. Hannah gasped. "Liam, it's gorgeous."

"It was my grandmother's. When I told Gramps I was going to propose, he gave it to me. Said he couldn't think of a better person to inherit Grandma's ring."

Tears rolled from her eyes as she held out her hand for him to slide it on.

Lacy stepped up to her side. "Wow. I guess it's a day for diamonds."

Ryan jumped down from the bed. "For the record, this is totally going in the show. This makes the final cut." He moved to Kayla's side and put an arm around her. He didn't say anything, but maybe something felt different this time, because Kayla looked up at him, and he looked down at her, and the way they smiled…

Hannah grinned and looked at the ring on her finger. A day for diamonds—and new beginnings.

She was glad someone had caught it on camera.

From the Author

Dear Reader,

When my husband decided to learn the film industry, TV-watching in my house went from a relaxing pastime to active research. While I was lost in the story being told, he was commenting on camera angles, musing about what lenses they were using, and grounding me in the how-to. We watched a ton of behind-the-scenes and the-making-of shows, and I listened as he told me all about the shoots he got to be on.

We both thought I'd mostly ignored his chatter. But when I sat down to write this story, I realized I'd retained more than I expected! It was pure fun to bring a fictional version of some of my favorite shows to life, albeit more simplified than it would really be, so it wasn't overwhelming.

And when I realized I'd get to write the proposal scene, there may have been some happy squealing from this romance-loving girl. My husband read the book as soon as I finished it to correct any film terminology that I got wrong, and he laughed at how I'd somehow managed to have *four* romances in this one little book. What can I say? Not sorry.

I hope you enjoyed this adventure in Blackberry Valley, the insight into what actually goes on behind the cameras of a television show, and most of all the many stories about how love finds us, whether it's romantic, familial, or that strong cord of friendship that can bind us despite distance or time.

Signed,
Roseanna

About the Author

Roseanna M. White is a bestselling, Christy Award-winning author who has long claimed that words are the air she breathes. Having successfully launched two homeschool grads, she now spends her time writing fiction, designing book covers, and pretending her house will clean itself. Roseanna is the author of a slew of historical novels that span several continents and thousands of years. Spies and war and mayhem always seem to find their way into her books… to offset her real life, which is blessedly ordinary.

The Hot Spotlight

Nestled in Barren County, Kentucky, is a geological wonderland. The region is known for its abundance of limestone, which not only lends itself to caves but also other fascinating geology. Unique crystal formations can be found in caves and rocks throughout the area. These crystals add a sparkling touch to the local geology, attracting amateur rock hounds and professional geologists alike.

Barren County is also rich in geodes, spherical rocks that contain a cavity lined with crystals or other minerals. These natural treasures are a delight to discover, especially for young explorers with a keen eye for geological wonders.

Fossil enthusiasts will also find Barren County intriguing, as the region boasts a rich fossil record. Fossils of ancient marine creatures, such as brachiopods, trilobites, and crinoids, can be unearthed in the limestone deposits of the area, offering a glimpse into the prehistoric past of Kentucky.

From the Hot Spot Kitchen

ORANGE DREAMS PIE
(ITALIAN RICE PIE)

Ingredients:

¾ cup powdered sugar

3 large eggs, room
  temperature

2 teaspoons vanilla

1 tablespoon orange zest

1 (15-ounce) tub whole milk
  ricotta

½ cup cooked short-grain rice

6 sheets phyllo dough

6 tablespoons butter, melted

Directions:

Preheat oven to 375 degrees and grease a 9-inch pie dish.

Blend powdered sugar, eggs, vanilla, orange zest, and ricotta in food processor or blender until smooth. Stir in cooked rice.

Lay one sheet of phyllo over pie dish, letting extra hang over edges equally on both sides. Brush with melted butter. Lay second sheet of dough at ninety degrees to the first and brush with butter as well. Continue with remaining sheets.

Pour ricotta mixture into dish. Fold sheets of dough over the filling to cover it completely. Brush top with melted butter.

Bake until dough is golden brown and filling is set, about 35 minutes. Cool completely. Garnish with a dusting of powdered sugar and serve. Leftovers should be stored in the refrigerator.

Read on for a sneak peek of another exciting book
in the *Mysteries of Blackberry Valley* series!

A Brush with Danger

BY BETH ADAMS

When Hannah Prentiss arrived at Bluegrass Hollow Farm, she saw that Liam Berthold's vehicle was already in the driveway. She smiled at the sight of her fiancé and his friend Archer Lestrade chatting outside the cottage with her best friend, Lacy Minyard.

Lacy waved at Hannah's car on the narrow lane. One hand rested on her round baby bump, while the other gestured at the cottage. She was upset about something—that was clear from the expression on her face. What was going on?

"Good morning," Hannah called through the open window as she parked beside Liam's Jeep. She grabbed the tray of coffees and the bag of bagels she'd picked up on the way over and hurried toward the group. Lacy's truck and a truck that must belong to contractor Gus Brody were also parked in the gravel parking area. A dumpster sat by the side of the house. The little cottage on the farm was tucked back into the woods, surrounded by beech and redbud trees, and even though its porch sagged and one of the gutters hung loose, it was a cute place. Or it would be, once the Minyards got done fixing it up.

"It's good to see you," Liam said, leaning over to kiss her cheek. She beamed as his lips brushed her skin. It had only been a few weeks since he'd proposed. Hannah had been told that she wouldn't always get butterflies when she saw the man she loved, but she was pretty sure she would. Anyone would, she thought as she took in Liam, standing there in his T-shirt and jeans with that goofy grin on his face, as if he couldn't believe his luck.

As if he were the lucky one.

"Hi, Hannah." Lacy stepped forward and leaned in for a hug. Hannah handed coffees and bagels to Archer, then hugged her back.

"Hi. What's going on?" Hannah asked, pulling back.

"The police are on their way," Lacy said.

"What? Why?"

Archer passed around the coffees, and Hannah took one gratefully. "The one marked *D* is for Lacy," she said. Archer nodded and held the decaf out for Lacy.

"You're always so thoughtful about my condition," Lacy said with a grateful smile. She took a sip from the cup and then gestured at the front window of the little cottage. "Someone broke in last night."

"Here?" Hannah felt foolish as soon as the word left her mouth. Of course here. But why would anyone break into this little cottage? There was nothing valuable inside. No one had lived there in years. Few people even knew the cottage existed, hidden in the woods a quarter mile from the main farmhouse.

"Gus brought some tools and equipment over yesterday so we could get started with demolition first thing this morning," Lacy explained. Liam had already told Hannah he and Archer volunteered to help with that process, which was why Hannah brought them breakfast. "But when we got here this morning, we found someone had smashed in the window and taken some of the tools. A power saw, a sledgehammer, and a full toolbox. They were sitting in the living room before, right inside this window."

"That's terrible." Hannah took a sip from her coffee, willing the caffeine to kick-start her brain. It was too early on a Saturday morning for puzzles. "But why? Who even knew they were there?"

"We don't know," Lacy said. "Gus is upset, obviously."

"Of course," Hannah said. "I would be too. Is he here?"

"He and Neil are both inside," Lacy said. Neil was her husband. "The rest of us are staying out of the crime scene until the police show up."

"Probably for the best," Hannah said. "But I don't understand. This cottage has been empty for how long?" The last time Hannah had been out here, in October, there was a padlock on the door. It was May now, and she doubted anyone had been here in the meantime.

"At least a dozen years," Lacy said. "No one has so much as touched the place in all that time."

"But as soon as you get ready to start renovating, someone smashes a window and steals the contractor's tools?" Hannah shook her head. "That timing is too weird."

"I know." Lacy took another sip of her coffee. "It makes no sense."

"The missing tools are valuable," Archer said. "Someone probably took them to sell."

Hannah turned her head at the sound of tires on gravel. A police car rumbled up the driveway. "Let's hope these guys can figure it out."

Deputies Alex and Jacky Holt, brother and sister, stepped out of the car. Neil came out onto the porch, followed by Gus Brody. Gus had graying brown hair and a mustache, and he wore dusty jeans and a heavy sweatshirt with work boots. He nodded a greeting to Hannah as he stepped off the porch.

"Look how cute this place is," Jacky said, walking a step ahead of her brother and eyeing the house. Her long brown hair was tied back in its usual ponytail. "How long has this cottage been here?"

"Forty years or so," Neil said. He was hardly a short man, but he seemed small standing next to the towering Liam and Archer.

"You've had a cottage here my whole life and I never knew about it?" Jacky demanded.

"My grandparents built it when my parents got married," Lacy said. "We're fixing it up so my mom can move into it, with the baby coming and all. Or rather, we're trying to. But someone had other plans." She gestured at the broken window.

"Let's take a look," Alex said.

While the deputies went inside the house, followed by Gus and the Minyards, Hannah sidled up next to Liam, who pulled her close to his side. He smelled like soap and aftershave, and she loved the feeling of his arm around her.

"I'm sorry you haven't gotten to destroy anything yet," Hannah said.

Liam and Archer would have been glad to help in any case, but they were especially excited to help demolish the old kitchen and bathroom in the cottage. Lacy and Neil were doing as much of the renovation work themselves as they could and bringing in Liam and Archer to help smash up unneeded cabinets and walls was a win-win. They didn't have to pay for professionals to demo the place, and Liam and Archer got to break things with sledgehammers.

"Oh, it's still happening," Liam said. "Don't worry. Once Gus gets that police report so he can file an insurance claim, we're up."

"The sledgehammer was taken, wasn't it?" Hannah asked.

"We brought our own," Archer said, grinning. "What do you think we are—amateurs?"

Hannah didn't know if sledgehammers were a tool firefighters used in their jobs or whether they both just happened to own them. Maybe both.

Archer and Liam started discussing a training drill the firefighters were preparing for the following week, and Archer mentioned a cavern he wanted to explore over in Cave City. Liam asked him about Brynn, Archer's fiancée, and then the deputies came back outside.

"Are there any clues as to who did this?" Liam asked as Alex walked down the steps.

"There's not a lot to go on, but we'll do our best," Jacky said.

"We dusted for fingerprints, but not much turned up," Alex said. "We'll check with the neighbors, see if anyone heard or saw anything."

"Good luck with that," Archer said, eyeing the thick trees around the cottage.

"We didn't hear or see anything, and we're the only neighbors within a mile," Neil said.

"We'll ask anyway. It's possible someone has doorbell cam footage of a car coming this way," Jacky said. "If there's a clue out there, we'll find it."

Hannah was confident Jacky was right, and she hoped they would find something. The deputies said goodbye and left.

"In the meantime, they say we can get to work," Neil said. "Since you guys brought your own tools."

Liam released Hannah, set his coffee on the hood of his Jeep, and then walked around it to open the rear door. A few minutes later, he and Archer strode toward the cottage with sledgehammers on their shoulders.

"Just the kitchen and bathroom!" Lacy called after them.

"No worries," Liam called back.

"Probably," Archer added.

"They are a little too excited about this," Lacy said.

"Of course they are," Neil said. "How often do they get permission to go into a house with a sledgehammer and break things? It's every guy's dream."

"I've got a spare hammer in my truck," Gus said, his eyes twinkling. "Do you want to join them, Neil?"

"I mean, I won't say no," Neil said. Hannah wanted to laugh. Neil owned a bookstore and adored antique maps, but he was still a boy at heart, just like the other two. A minute later, Neil disappeared inside with his own sledgehammer, and soon they heard the first crash coming from inside the house, followed by the sound of wood splintering.

"I hope that was something that was supposed to break," Lacy said with a laugh.

There was another crash, and the sound of the men cheering and laughing.

"You want to join them?" Gus asked Hannah. "I might have another sledgehammer in my truck."

"No thank you," Hannah said, holding up her hands. "I'm here for moral support."

"Suit yourself." Gus shrugged and headed toward the house. There was another smash, and then a thud, and then a couple of raised voices.

A moment later, Neil appeared in the doorway. "Lacy? You may want to come take a look at this."

Lacy and Hannah both rushed to the door. Lacy tugged a dust mask over her face, then handed another to Hannah.

The air was choked with dust, and from the doorway Hannah could see that most of the kitchen cabinets already lay in ruins on the floor. The wall behind the top cabinets in the kitchen had been opened, and the drywall lay in pieces on top of the cabinets. The drywall on the exterior wall had giant gaps in it as well. The studs were exposed, and now that she got close, Hannah could see why they had stopped.

"This stuff was hidden behind the wall," Archer said. "We thought it might be important."

Hannah leaned forward, trying to make sense of what she was seeing. "What is that?"

Something was wedged between the studs, a rectangle wrapped in brown paper. And above it was a cylinder wrapped in the same paper.

Lacy pulled out the rectangle and tore off the paper. "What in the world?" It looked like some kind of painting. It was small, less than a foot wide and tall, and it showed a lush landscape. An elaborate gold-colored frame surrounded it.

Liam unrolled the second paper and found a canvas showing a bunch of animals and people standing around together. It looked as if it had been roughly cut from its frame.

"Lacy," Hannah said, "why are there paintings hidden in the wall in your cottage?"

Lacy shook her head. "Your guess is as good as mine."

Loved *Mysteries of Blackberry Valley?*
Check out some other Guideposts mystery series!

Whistle Stop Café Mysteries

Join best friends Debbie Albright and Janet Shaw as they step out in faith to open the Whistle Stop Café inside the historic train depot in Dennison, Ohio. During WWII, the depot's canteen workers offered doughnuts, sandwiches, and a heap of gratitude to thousands of soldiers on their way to war via troop-transport trains. Our sleuths soon find themselves on track to solve baffling mysteries—both past and present. Come along for the ride for stories of honor, duty to God and country, and of course fun, family, and friends!

Under the Apple Tree
As Time Goes By
We'll Meet Again
Till Then
I'll Be Seeing You
Fools Rush In
Let It Snow
Accentuate the Positive
For Sentimental Reasons

That's My Baby

A String of Pearls

Somewhere Over the Rainbow

Down Forget-Me-Not Lane

Set the World on Fire

When You Wish Upon a Star

Rumors Are Flying

Here We Go Again

Stairway to the Stars

Winter Weather

Wait Till the Sun Shines

Now You're in My Arms

Sooner or Later

Apple Blossom Time

My Dreams Are Getting Better

Secrets from Grandma's Attic

Life is recorded not only in decades or years, but in events and memories that form the fabric of our being. Follow Tracy Doyle, Amy Allen, and Robin Davisson, the granddaughters of the recently deceased centenarian, Pearl Allen, as they explore the treasures found in the attic of Grandma Pearl's Victorian home, nestled near the banks of the Mississippi in Canton, Missouri. Not only do Pearl's descendants uncover a long-buried mystery at every attic exploration, they also discover their grandmother's legacy of deep, abiding faith, which has shaped and guided their family through the years. These uncovered Secrets from Grandma's Attic reveal stories of faith, redemption, and second chances that capture your heart long after you turn the last page.

The Prince and the Popper

Something Shady

Duel Threat

A Royal Tea

The Heart of a Hero

Fractured Beauty

A Shadowy Past

In Its Time

Nothing Gold Can Stay

The Cameo Clue

Veiled Intentions

Turn Back the Dial

A Marathon of Kindness

A Thief in the Night

Coming Home

A Note from the Editors

We hope you enjoyed another exciting volume in the Mysteries of Blackberry Valley series, published by Guideposts. For over seventy-five years, Guideposts, a nonprofit organization, has been driven by a vision of a world filled with hope. We aspire to be the voice of a trusted friend, a friend who makes you feel more hopeful and connected.

By making a purchase from Guideposts, you join our community in touching millions of lives, inspiring them to believe that all things are possible through faith, hope, and prayer. Your continued support allows us to provide uplifting resources to those in need. Whether through our communities, websites, apps, or publications, we inspire our audiences, bring them together, and comfort, uplift, entertain, and guide them. Visit us at guideposts.org to learn more.

We would love to hear from you. Write us at Guideposts, P.O. Box 5815, Harlan, Iowa 51593 or call us at (800) 932-2145. Did you love *The Final Cut*? Leave a review for this product on guideposts.org/shop. Your feedback helps others in our community find relevant products.

Find inspiration, find faith, find Guideposts.

Shop our best sellers and favorites at
guideposts.org/shop
Or scan the QR code to go directly to our Shop

More Great Mysteries
Are Waiting For Readers Like *You*!

Whistle Stop Café Mysteries

"Memories of a lifetime...I loved reading this story. Could not put the book down...." —ROSE H.

Mystery and WWII historical fiction fans will love these intriguing novels where two close friends piece together clues to solve mysteries past and present. Set in the real town of Dennison, Ohio, at a historic train depot where many soldiers once set off for war, these stories are filled with faithful, relatable characters you'll love spending time with.

Mysteries & Wonders of the Bible

"I so enjoyed this book....What a great insight into the life of the women who wove the veil for the Temple." —SHIRLEYN J.

Have you ever wondered what it might have been like to live back in Bible times to experience miraculous Bible events firsthand? Then you'll LOVE the fascinating **Mysteries & Wonders of the Bible** novels! Each Scripture-inspired story whisks you back to the ancient Holy Land, where you'll accompany ordinary men and women in their search for the hidden truths behind some of the most pivotal moments in the Bible. Each volume includes insights from a respected biblical scholar to help you ponder the significance of each story to your own life.

Mysteries of Cobble Hill Farm

"Wonderful series. Great story. Spellbinding. Could not put it down once I started reading." —BONNIE C.

Escape to the charming English countryside with **Mysteries of Cobble Hill Farm**, a heartwarming series of faith-filled mysteries. Harriet Bailey relocates to Yorkshire, England, to take over her late grandfather's veterinary practice, hoping it's the fresh start she needs. As she builds a new life, Harriet uncovers modern mysteries and long-buried secrets in the village and among the rolling hills and castle ruins. Each book is an inspiring puzzle where God's gentlest messengers—the animals in her care—help Harriet save the day.

Learn More & Shop These Exciting Mysteries, Biblical Stories, & Other Uplifting Fiction at **guideposts.org/fiction**